Gloria, AAUW + Swimming Buddy,

Laraine Asper Minier

10-2004

Cover picture: *After School*, Harvey Dunn, 1950, compliments of the South Dakota Art Museum.

When visiting the Art Museum in Brookings, I was utterly charmed by the painting "After School" by Harvey Dunn, South Dakota's distinguished painter.

The school and outhouse are the exact images of the school my ten siblings and I had attended through eighth grade.

The pupils rushing for home carrying their empty syrup can dinner pails are just like the ones we had used. The blue sky filled with fluffy clouds, the dry coarse sod, and the barbed wire fence separating a field from the school captures the essence of the South Dakota prairie landscape.

WAYWARD WINDS OF THE '30s
The Asper Family Saga
by
Lorraine Asper Minier

Tell me the landscape in which you live, and I will tell you who you are.

—Jose Ortega y Gasser

This sense of planet allows Dakotans to feel as if they are in the middle of the world rather than, as others would have it, in the middle of nowhere. The longer Europeans remain in America, the more Indian they will become. What makes an Indian an Indian is a deep connection to the land built over generations that imbues their psychology and eventually their spirituality and makes them one with the spirit of the land.

—Paul Gunn, Native American

Library of Congress Control Number: 2004097013

ISBN: 1-57579-292-3

First printing 2004

Printed in the United States of America
PINE HILL PRESS
4000 West 57th Street
Sioux Falls, SD 57106

Preface

In May of 1994, during a restless night, I came to the conclusion that I needed to write a family memoir for my four sons and their children. They had never asked questions or shown any curiosity about my childhood, but I felt that as they grew older, when their lives were no longer dictated by work and children, they would want to know about my early life and could compare it to their own.

As a young person, I, too, had never been curious about my parents' early life. And now, it seemed too late. My father, mother and older siblings were dead leaving me with so many unanswered questions. So, I decided I would write a memoir, a history of the Asper family, not only for my immediate family but also for my brothers' and sisters' children and all our progeny. I knew I would have to do a lot of searching to get the facts, but it sounded interesting and challenging. I decided early on that I would focus on the family during the 1930s. I'd show how each one coped during this time of the Great Depression.

My life was molded by two major factors. The first was my position in the family. I am the eleventh child, born when my parents were 50 and 49, near their twenty-fifth wedding anniversary! My siblings ranged from seven to 24 years older. I was always around those many years older than I; thus, in my early years I related more to adults than to those my own age. The second factor was being born in 1927 on the eve of the Depression and shortly before the great drought and dust storms ruined the land.

During these ten years, time seemed almost at a stand still. It was impossible to progress. Resources were limited. Day to day existence consumed the farmer's energy. My father, Hans, who had been so proud to be a farmer, saw himself as an independent entity, completely in charge of his own business. But several years of crop failures and low stock prices reduced him and the family to a level of poverty he had never known. He had mortgaged and remortgaged his holdings. He stood to lose the land he had fashioned with his own hands, heart and imagination. He believed he was working with God, his wife and family to capture the American Dream, but these years brought him to the brink of disaster.

Dedication

This book is dedicated to all those mid-western farmers who lived on the plains and fought a constant war with their environment. They were truly heroes in the 1930s engaged in an unending battle that lasted for ten arduous years.

The farmer was the soldier who every day faced his enemy, the harsh elements of the South Dakota plains. There were the devastating winds that blew the good topsoil away, some traced as far as the East Coast. These strong, dry winds contributed to the drought. When the rains did come it was often at the wrong time and never enough. There were also blighted wheat crops from rust along with the grasshoppers that came in great droves and devoured the inferior crops and even ate the clothes on the drying lines!

In the area of business, the farmer felt helpless and angry when banks closed and he lost his small savings. He was sorely disappointed by the return on his scant crops. His returns barely paid for the seed and manpower it took to produce. He was frightened by the possibility of foreclosure on his mortgage. If this happened, it could mean he and his family would have to move, but where and for what kind of work?

Even the government that was trying to help by introducing work programs such as Works Progress Administration (WPA), seemed demeaning. To Hans and his fellow farmers, this was give-away relief that proud plain's people could not readily accept. All of these fears plagued him along with the physical backbreaking work that wore him out by day's end.

It is hard to imagine the turmoil of fear, grief, anger and terror that must have stormed through the farmer's frustrated soul daily. Yet, he had to rise each morning to face another day courageously for the sake of his loved ones, knowing that possible failure dogged his every footstep.

This saga is the story of HANS ASPER, a true plain's farmer, who along with his wife, Milda, and family fought with the elements, but who bravely and unwaveringly carried on their battle despite the destructive forces that attempted to defeat them and their fellow farmers.

Dakota Land Song

We do not live, we only stay
We are too poor to get away.

Why do people stay on this land?

1. Inertia: unable to make any decision after so long a time of unclear thinking.
2. Home: not a house, not land but "home," family, familiarity and extended family.
3. Lack of money: can't sell land or personal belongings to get a "grubstake."
4. Lack of knowledge of a place where things might be better. They had thought this place was better and look what happened!
5. Pride: I did this on my own. I was so sure it was right. I put my entire life and soul into this land and now I must acknowledge I made a mistake.

Plains people were drawn by the "enchantment of the prairie." The scorched, stunted fields from drought opened great cracks in the dry earth – this land that had seemed so fertile! It was necessary to adapt grains for the short growing season and the extreme dry conditions that ruined the crops.

Men and women on the prairie endured storms of all sorts – great discomforts and disaster for all their lives while attempting to conquer their land.

from *Land of the Burnt Thigh*
by Edith Eudora Kohl

The Effects of the 1929
Depression on South Dakotans

The Great Depression was a traumatic experience for all Americans as the preceding years had been quite comfortable ones and Americans, in general, were optimistic. Everyone felt that this was a New Era where everyone could prosper. However, South Dakota farmers did not have this same feeling as they had been struggling since the early '20s when the economy had bottomed out for them.

From BLACK THURSDAY, October 25, 1929, when the Stock Market in the U.S. crashed, it took almost 12 years of very slow growth for the country to recover. For the mid-west farmer, it was more like 25 years. After WWI ended in 1918, agriculture prices dropped quickly, so the state had to float bonds so banks could stay open. The state of South Dakota was in debt 47 million dollars, a huge debt for such a small state! It would take the state 25 years to pay off this debt! Then in 1924, there was another recession and banks were closed, taking many depositors' small savings, and then again in 1929 when the Crash came, the banks closed again leaving them with no money even to buy seed for next springs planting. Hence, these people lost trust in the government and banking institutions. They had nothing to look forward to but paying off their past debts and additional taxes to cover the state's debt.

The mid-west farmers had always been very self-reliant. They bought large acreages knowing that through their hard work, they could produce enough to sell or trade for what they needed. They were a proud group most being somewhere between first or second generation Americans who must

55 Artesian Students Eat At School Lunch Room

Artesian, S. D.—(Special)—This is a picture of the lunch room in local school, where 55 country pupils are served a hot lunch each school day. This is maintained as a WPA project with two local women in charge. These pupils, otherwise, would have to eat a cold lunch brought from home.

have felt they had conquered this wonderful wide open country they loved in comparison to the countries their forefathers had migrated from. But their lack of control of all kinds of unexpected circumstances soon made these South Dakota farmers very wary. Their opposition was not only the government, but nature itself. There was the rainfall. When it did come, there was never enough or it came at the wrong time. Winters were extremely cold and the summers were so hot they burned the crops in the fields. Then the grasshoppers came in hoards eating everything in their way – even the sheets on the wash line! Dry winds blew the topsoil away, hence came the repugnant name, THE DIRTY THIRTIES.

Not only were the farmers suffering, but the entire population of the United States and for that matter all the world were in a deep stage economic depression. Europe could no longer buy U.S. grains. The grain elevators across America were full, so there was little market for the farmer's goods. According to historians, South Dakota was one of the hardest hit states. It was time for the government to step in to prepare some plans to aid America's stricken population.

In 1932, Franklin Roosevelt became president. He knew drastic actions had to be taken to help these destitute Americans. In his first speeches, he stated, "The only thing we have to fear is fear itself." He worked with the Senators and Representatives to hurriedly get some programs going to alleviate these great problems. He named these programs the NEW DEAL. His major idea was to create work projects for the people. The government could just pass out welfare checks, but he felt working for their wages was far better for the worker's morale. 8.5 million people benefited from these programs.

A part of the NEW DEAL was WPA which stood for Work Projects Administration. This agency hired workers in every state to build roads, parks, bridges, swimming pools, even hot lunch programs for students to make sure that these children had at least one good meal a day.

The WPA also created jobs in the arts. Murals were painted on walls of important buildings. Plays and concerts were written for actors and musicians then performed. In small towns like Artesian, teachers gave piano and elocution lessons to young students. They were paid by the WPA.

Camera Shots

All the pictures in this book will be in black and white as that was the only Kodak film available in the 30s. We had one inexpensive box camera. Since we had no trees, flowers or a lawn, in most of our pictures we are either standing in front of the house or by a car. If a person posed facing the West, you'd see the vast empty treeless plains in the East as a background. We were usually dressed in our newest or best outfits, ready to go to church or to town for shopping.

Table of Contents

Preface v
Dedication...vi
Dakota Land Song vii
The Effects of the 1929 Depression on South Dakotans ix
Acknowledgments xiii

Hans Theodore Asper (1877-1958) 1
    Social Events at the Turn of the Century 5
Milda Hanson Asper (1878-1973) 7
    In Loving Memory 12
    Bibelen 13
Avis Marcella Asper (1903-1996) 15
    Home, Home on the Range..18
Harvey Clayton Asper (1905-1957)..21
    Automobiles 25
Leo Paul Asper, the Quiet Man (1906-1969)..27
    Leo, the Thresher 30
    Dirty Thirties..33
Vernie Burdette Asper (1908-1992)..35
    Hi Ho the Dairy O! 39
Florence Louise Asper (1910-   ) 43
    This is the House that Hans Built 47
    The Paradox of the Close Family 50
Margery Hortense Asper (1912-1994)...51
Ernest Wilbert Asper (1914-1960)..54
    Tobacco 58
Helen Pauline Asper (1915-   ) 59
    Saturday Night Bath 63
Dale Raymond Asper (1917-2004) 67
    Cars and Roads and Roads and Cars 70
Russell Eugene Asper (1920-   ) 73
    Gold Medal Baby 77
Lorraine Eloyce Asper (1927-   ) 79
    A Place at the Table...85
Ole Remmen—Our Norwegian Bachelor 87
Privy Information..89
Artesian—Our Town 91
Grandma Asper's Cookie Recipes 97
Asper Family Health Chart 101
Asper—Geneology 103
Hanson-Helmey Geneology..112
Bibliography: Norwegian Writings 114

WWII Military Service 115
    Our Three Star Flag..117
    Ernest, the Navy Man 119
    Dale, Army Air Corps 123
    Russell, Navy Air Corps 127

List of Illustrations

Map of Norway Township 4
Map of South Dakota...41
Map of Oneida Township..49
Map of Norway 102

Acknowledgments

Mange tusen takk   **Many thousand thanks**

To son, Lon and wife Gail, for their technical support and the countless hours they spent preparing my script for the publishers.

To my South Dakota friend, Liz Doyle, who skillfully and nostalgically edited all of my stories.

To my niece, Teresa Asper Anderson, for her fine editing of the biographies of all her Asper aunts and uncles.

To my dear husband, Norman, who read every first draft and countless revisions with awe and inspiring words!

To my brother, Russ and wife Jerry, whose seven years' seniority added much needed insights about our family and various events of the 1930s.

To my Daughters of Norway Writing Group who for five years listened to countless stories adding bits from their own experiences. And especially to our leader, Cherle Stephenson, who kept us all on course.

To my Seattle cousins, Al and Hazel Asper Smith, who updated the family genealogy to June 30, 2004.

To my friend, Paul Duffield, now deceased, who gave me information on the pay scale for WPA workers.

To Roland Powell for his exquisite sketches of the thrashing scenes.

To my benefactors:

My nephew, Gary and wife Mary Lukehart, who said to me, "The Asper family and farm should be written about." I replied, "I'll write the book if you finance the publishing," and so it came to be.

My nephew, Mark and my brother Dale, for their financial contribution. Unfortunately, Dale died May 26, 2004 before the book was published, but he had read several of my stories and especially liked the one about his military service in India flying the "Hump."

Hans Theodore and Milda Hanson Asper
November 26, 1902

Hans Theodore Asper (1877 - 1958)

My father, Hans Theodore Asper, was born July 4, 1877, in Lincoln County, South Dakota. He was a first generation American as his father, Karl Larsen Asper, and Karl's brother August came to America in the mid-1860s. The brothers worked for a few years, then returned to Norway to marry Norwegian girls. Karl married Anne Amundsdatter Sulerud and they returned to the United States and settled in Lincoln County, in the southeastern part of South Dakota. There, Hans was born, their third child.

Hans grew up steeped in Old Northern European culture. Of course, Norwegian was his first language. He lived in Norway Township, a region totally immersed with hundreds of other Norwegian immigrants. There was a Lutheran church every three miles and Hans attended Lands Norwegian Lutheran Church, where all services were conducted in Norwegian and where his baptismal and confirmation certificates were issued in Norwegian. Throughout his life, Hans carried his ancestry with great pride and always showed an interest in the heritage of others.

Hans's assimilation into American culture began when he started school. Here he learned to speak and write English (although he knew how to read Norwegian as well). He was good in arithmetic and had beautiful penmanship. His mastery of the fundamental three R's stood him in good stead for his future life as a farmer. Unfortunately, he was only able to attend school until fifth grade.

Next came the mastery of farming. Just imagine taking on the responsibilities of an adult at the age of twelve. One can hardly realize the arduous tasks that this very young boy was undertaking. He was only one of many young farm boys who had to forsake school to help in the fields to eke out a living for their large families. At that time, children were assets and proud to help their parents so their farm would prosper.

The Karl Asper family was growing, so there were many little mouths to feed. In fifteen years, nine children were born! My dad was used to being surrounded by many children, so later when Hans had his own large family there were few surprises for him. We know little about life in Karl's family except we can surmise a strong religious element and firm discipline. Karl's wife Anne never adjusted to life in the United States. Surely this must have been troublesome for the family when the wife and mother, the very center of the home, was so unhappy. Anne was only fifty when she died.

Although Hans had to work hard, he had time to attend church and sing in the choir. He had a very good voice and loved music. He made good friends at church and enjoyed social events at other members' homes. No doubt this is where he met his future wife, Milda Hanson, a member of the choir and its accompanist.

Hans worked for his father and as he grew older, he worked for other neighboring farmers as well. After marrying Milda in 1902, he started farming full time for others and they considered his services excellent. He became anxious to buy his own farm. Since land was expensive where he lived, he bought more reasonably priced land in Sanborn County, about 130 miles to the northwest. In 1910, Hans and Milda moved to a small two-room house he'd had built for them there. Their first crops were very good, so three years later Hans had a large farmhouse built for their growing family, paying $4,000 in cash. He surely must have felt proud to have achieved so much so quickly. Of course by 1914, the United States had entered World War I, so farmers received good prices for the grain and livestock they contributed to the war effort. In the early 1920s, there was a depression and the banks closed, bringing on a recession. Times got a little better through the mid-twenties. Then in October 1929, the stock market crashed which absolutely devastated the entire country. In the early thirties, a great drought began which brought the country into even more straitened circumstances.

This is where Hans found himself in the early thirties. He'd been married twenty-eight years and had eleven children, most of whom lived at home. The terrible rolling dust storms blew the topsoil away far too often, and there was little rain or no rain at the right time. Kathleen Norris in her book, *Dakota*, explains:

> "Until I moved to western South Dakota, I did not know about rain, that it could come too hard, too soft, too hot, too cold, too early, too late. That there could be too little at the right time, too much at the wrong time and vice versa. I did not know that a light rain coming at the end of a hot afternoon, with the temperature at 100 degrees or more, can literally burn wheat, steaming it on the stalk so it's not worth harvesting. I had not seen a long, slow rain come at harvest making grain lying in the swath begin to sprout again, ruining it as a cash crop. I had not realized that a long soaking rain in spring or fall, a straight-down-falling rain, a gentle, splashing rain is more than a blessing. It's a miracle."

Although Norris is writing about a different time period and a different area of South Dakota, her observations are perfectly appropriate to what happened in the Midwest during the early to mid-thirties. Hans endured all these rain traumas. He planted crops for seven years with very little harvest – sometimes not enough to even pay for the seed! The rains were either too early or too late, or there was no rain, or the sun baked everything or the grasshoppers ate what little was left.

The faithful must have wondered what they'd done wrong to deserve such unmerciful treatment, reminiscent of the scourges God sent to punish the Egyptians, when their only desire was to till the earth, to bring forth crops, and to feed their families and others from their beloved land. Many families just gave up under all this strain and drifted off somewhere. But Hans had too much invested in money and in toil on his farm, he could not let it go. He mortgaged the farm twice. The government established the Federal Land Bank to aid ailing farmers. This New Deal program helped the farmer by rescinding some of his debt and decreasing his mortgage payment by amortizing the loan over a longer period. This aid assisted many farmers, as well as Hans, who was able to keep his farm.

Along with all the other handicaps life had thrown his way during the drought, Hans contracted anthrax. Two of his cows died of anthrax so he burned them twice each day so as to rid the herd of this horrible disease. Perhaps it was the smoke fumes that reached his lungs that caused his illness. Anthrax kept him in bed for several months, but he finally recovered and was slowly able go back to his usual work schedule.

By 1938, weather conditions started to improve and farming slowly became profitable again. The entire nation was coming out of the Depression and the economy was on the upward swing. By 1940, war was looming in Europe with a likelihood the United States would be joining in the fight. Prices were rising and it appeared that the country was healing again after such a long wearisome period that would not soon be forgotten.

Looking back on the long life of Hans Asper (d.1958), we see a man of great dignity and character who fashioned a life for himself and his family far beyond what might have been expected from his limited education. He was a skilled farmer and his farm was carefully planned and laid out in a most practical manner. He brought up six sons and five daughters who exceeded his expectations and of whom he was proud in their various vocations. He was able to redeem his farm, sell it for a good profit and eventually retire with his wife to Artesian where they lived very happily in retirement.

MAP OF NORWAY TOWNSHIP

Birthplace of Hans Asper (34)
Milda Hanson (24)
Lands Lutheran Church

Social Events at the Turn of the Century

Hans and Milda were in their early 20s at the turn of the 19th century. What did the young folks do for entertainment in those days? They went to church and, no doubt, their favorite activity was the once a week choir practice. My father was a good singer. My mother sang, too, but was also the church pianist. So their Lutheran church must have been their courting ground.

There is a beautiful photograph of this choir. In it are several of my father's sisters and cousins, my mother's best friend, Emma, and, of course, Hans and Milda. The choir members are all in their very best clothes. The men wear three-piece suits with neckties, their hair medium long with no beards. The photographer has placed the women in front on low stools carefully arranging their long skirts and long hair neatly arranged. They wear no make-up and appear withdrawn, revealing little of themselves. They are Norwegian, always circumspect. They never draw attention to themselves!

But they were stirred into action when they sang the beautiful sacred music. How wonderful they must have felt raising their voices in four-part

Front Row - L to R - Emma Rossum, Milda (Grubbrud) Knutson, Rachel (Rogness) Boyd. Middle Row - L to R - Ovidia (Asper) Roberts, Carl Hagen, Nettie (Asper) Hagen. Lewis Asper, Emma (Asper) Ulberg. Back Row - L to R - Milda (Hanson) Asper, Hans Asper, Emil Rogness, Aletha (Asper) Rogness

5

harmony singing in praise to the Lord. They are all Lutherans, all baptized, all confirmed and all to be married and buried in this faith that was brought by their parents from the old country.

Other church activities, besides Sunday services, would be special meetings when visiting pastors or missionaries came to speak. Ladies-Aid would meet once a month for Bible Study. There were the occasional funerals, picnics and seasonal celebrations.

Most other social functions centered around the home. Friends might stop by in their buggies in the afternoon and partake of a Norwegian repast, and the preacher would make his obligatory call twice a year. All would be served a special Norwegian coffee made with eggshells. Coffee and eggshells were mixed and boiled together which produced a very smooth drink. Perhaps there would be hearty sandwiches as well as several kinds of Norwegian delicacies such as Spritz cookies, Krum Kake, Sandbakelse, Berlinerkranser, Rosettes or Fattigman. All of these creations are very rich since they contain a lot of butter and eggs with just a little flour.

If a visitor came on the right day he might get there for lefse making! Lefse is the national bread of Norway and a specialty of transplanted Norskies in the U.S. Lefse is made from mashed potatoes along with a bit of shortening and flour and served rolled with butter and a sprinkling of sugar. This would be a treat at an impromptu afternoon coffee party. On holidays, meatballs or lutefisk would be rolled up tightly into the lefse and consumed with much delight!

When these parties were in the home, no one drank hard liquor or smoked or danced. They probably visited, played games, sang and ate the good hearty food.

Another social event my mother spoke of fondly was the Chautauqua. This was a lecture series that came around on rare occasions. A tent would be pitched in one of the larger towns, wherein lectures would be given on a variety of topics. The series would last for several days. Mother was always open to learning new things.

Now, I'm thinking about the great contrast in entertainment one hundred years later. The young people of today usually go outside of their homes for entertainment. Perhaps some attend a rock concert where the decibels are at the highest levels! The musicians whirl in wild abandon in colorful, unbelievable duds or lack there of! Their hair is long, unkempt and probably of various colors. The clothes, hair and behavior cry out for attention! Favorite foods are chips, dips, pizza and many other compositional foods – no fresh homemade food that nourishes the body and the brain like in great-grandpappy's day. Young people are receivers not participants like their forefathers. Well, that's "progress;" who's to stop it!

Milda Hanson Asper (1878 - 1973)

My mother, Milda Hanson, grew up in southeastern South Dakota in a Norwegian community in Lincoln County, Norway Township. She was a first generation American whose parents had arrived in the United States in the 1850s. Her family clung to their old country ways, including speaking Norwegian and attending the Norwegian Lutheran church, while settling into this new and wonderful country to which they had immigrated. Milda was the youngest child in the family, having five older brothers and two older sisters.

Although Norwegian was spoken at home, Milda probably learned some English from her older siblings before she started

Milda Hanson Asper

country school. Her formal education was completed at the eighth grade. After this, she was sent to Sioux Falls for a year to take piano lessons from the nuns at the convent. She practiced many hours a day using her time efficiently in order to become proficient at the piano. While in Sioux Falls, she stayed with the Johnson's who ran a shoe store. Mrs. Johnson was her cousin. Upon returning home, she gave music lessons to those few neighbors owning a piano or pump organ, traveling to her students' homes in her horse and buggy. On another occasion, Milda took sewing lessons in Sioux Falls. She became a skilled seamstress – so much so she made her own beautiful silk wedding gown. Later her sewing ability would be very useful in making and patching clothes for her many children.

Milda sang in the church choir and was their pianist as well. It was at choir practice at Moe Lutheran Church that she became acquainted with a handsome young man, Hans Asper. They courted and were married on November 26, 1902. Milda was 24 years old at the time of her marriage; back then, people probably considered her an old maid. Hans was a year older.

Hans and Milda spent their first eight years together in Norway Township where Hans farmed for other people. They had their first four children there – Avis, Harvey, Leo and Vernie. As comfortable as it was to live near their family and friends, they decided they needed to get their own farm. Land was cheaper farther west, so they followed the general westward trend of the country and moved to Sanborn County, about 130 miles away. Hans had a small two-room house built for them until he had harvested a few good crops so they could afford to build a larger house. Florence was the first child born after their move and Margery followed about two years later. The walls of that little house must have been bursting with the noise and activity of six young children. It's hard to imagine the winters when the children would have to stay inside and Mother would have to deal with keeping them content as well as the cooking and laundry, including diapers for at least two children. My mother must have had nerves of steel and unstinting energy to keep up with all of this; she truly was a pioneer woman.

Mother must have felt like a queen in her castle when their new house was built – five bedrooms, an indoor bathroom, large kitchen, dining room, living room and full basement. Built in 1913, the new home was modern for a farmhouse. It had a coal furnace in the basement with registers sending heat to all rooms. There was a full bathroom with hot and cold running water at a time when most farmers had to carry water from their well to the house and heat it on the stove. A unique feature of the house was a special cupboard between the kitchen and dining room that could be accessed from either side. Built into this cupboard was a dumb waiter that allowed one to lower food to the basement level for cooling between meals.

My mother successfully handled the work involved in raising a large family that eventually included eleven children. She was well organized and would plan each day carefully. She stuck by the old rule of washing on Monday, ironing on Tuesday, cleaning on Friday, going to town on Saturday for trading and church on Sunday.

When making cakes or cookies, she'd line up the ingredients on the kitchen table, then sit down with a bowl and spoon and stir. This gave her a much-needed rest. She'd place items that needed to go upstairs on the steps, so whoever was going up would take them and put them in their proper place. Her favorite motto was "What's worth doing is worth doing well." In a different time or place she could have become an efficiency expert. Watching our mother work was a great learning experience for us children as we absorbed her methods and later applied them in our own lives.

Mother was a very good, though plain cook. She'd buy two small onions a month so you know we weren't over spiced! About three times a week, mother baked wonderful bread and rolls that usually came out of the oven just as we were arriving home from school. The aroma sent our salivary glands into high gear and we could hardly wait to wrap our mouths around that fresh bread and homemade butter! She liked feeding her family good wholesome foods and getting new recipes. She was an extremely frugal person. No food ever went to waste in her house; she could find some use for even one cold boiled potato. Eric Severid said about his Norwegian mother, "She'd make a Scotch woman look like a spendthrift." That fit my mother exactly.

Sadly, my mother didn't have any close women friends to provide mutual support and friendship through these years of pregnancy and childrearing. Her mother and sisters lived far away and although Hans tried to help out, he had his own burdens providing for their burgeoning family. Mother occasionally did have help from Norwegian immigrant girls who would work for room and board until they moved on or were married. Hans helped in bathing the children and putting them to bed, something he could do at night after his chores were done.

Mother had a serious demeanor; we seldom saw her smile or act light hearted. She wasn't unhappy or depressed, but just approached each day's agenda in a grave and businesslike manner. During the worst part of the Depression, when everyone was feeling down with economic worries, mother continued with her daily tasks, seemingly emotionless. She said that she was worried but always appeared calm. We never saw her cry. She often stated that she "never complained," refusing to waste time on such a negative action. Probably her stoic nature was part of the Norwegian heritage inherited from her immigrant parents. Several members of our family have appropriated mother's appearance of seriousness.

Most housewives of the day wore homemade cotton housedresses and aprons they had fashioned and sewed themselves, and good sturdy shoes. My mother wore the same. For a Saturday night in town or for church, mother owned one good dress, a black hat and black dress-up shoes. When going to town, she'd apply a little powder to her face which was the extent of her makeup. She never wore her lovely wide gold wedding band because water would get under it doing daily chores and perhaps later in life it became too tight for her finger. Mother wore her thin hair stretched tightly back and gathered into a small bun held by bone hairpins.

With mother's daily agenda of cooking and baking and other chores, she had little time for outdoor activities. She also felt that the outdoor chores were the domain of her husband and sons. Only occasionally, when there was no one to collect the eggs, she would go out to the chicken coop to do that chore. She did have her own little businesses, such as selling buttermilk to our doctor, home-churned butter to friends, eggs and spring chickens in season. Mother would hatch or buy baby chicks very early in the spring and struggle to keep them alive in a brooder house with a kerosene stove that kept them warm, as spring was still chilly for these baby chicks. When the chickens were ready to market, the town folk would drive to the farm and purchase spring chickens for one dollar each. She also culled out the old hens that were not laying and they would quickly become next Sunday's dinner.

Mother loved to go to Lutheran Ladies Aid meetings. This was her one opportunity for socialization with other women. Once a month, in the afternoon, the Aid would meet for Bible study and prayer. Then they would plan their monthly Saturday night suppers for the public. These affairs helped raise money for such church expenses as the minister's salary, coal and upkeep on the manse and church. The supper menu usually featured chicken or beef supplied by the farm wives. Each fall, they hosted a pheasant dinner with the game supplied by local hunters. The annual Christmas dinner included lutefisk and lefse. The women had to buy the lutefisk, but everything else was supplied by the Aid members. They charged twenty-five cents a plate for this great homemade food. Times being as hard as they were, not everyone had a quarter to take advantage of these delicious home cooked meals.

The ladies worked hard on these evenings, but enjoyed their sisterhood as they worked and laughed together. Mom would be so excited after this experience she would talk all the way home. She knew all the latest gossip, such as how the two women who didn't get along had been assigned to work in different rooms. She found all this delightful and could hardly wait for the next month's church supper to roll around!

When mother had some free time, playing the piano came first on her list of things to do. Every Sunday night she would play and sing hymns with dad. When they finally got a radio, she enjoyed listening to "Ma Perkins" while resting in the afternoon and to "Fibber McGee and Molly" and Jack Benny in the evening. I don't remember her ever reading – she might have been afraid of getting caught up in the story and not getting back to her work. She also liked quilting bees, an infrequent event but another lovely time for her with lady friends.

My mother was a strong believer in education. I'm sure she must have been disappointed her older children weren't able to attend high school. But she managed to send Avis and Margery to Augustana Normal School to become teachers, Helen to nurses' training at the Methodist Hospital, and Russ and me to college where we both received degrees. These were very proud moments for both mother and dad.

By the time she reached her fifties, mother began to feel the strain of her overburdened life and got to a point where she could not get out of bed. She started receiving treatments for her back from an osteopath in order to walk. Mother was later diagnosed with angina, a mild heart condition that would occasionally force her to rest in bed for a day to replenish her strength. She had high blood pressure too, but on the whole, once she reached her sixties and all her children were raised, and times had improved, her health improved. When mother and dad retired from the farm and moved into Artesian, they were able to relax and enjoy their retirement. They were like different people. Dad developed a good sense of humor and mother appeared much more relaxed and even learned to smile! She enjoyed making cookies, cinnamon rolls and other goodies for her grandchildren who lived near by.

As the youngest of eleven children, my upbringing was different than that of my siblings. Mother was 49 when I was born, and I think she was just worn out by parenting. I didn't receive bedtime stories, hugs or kisses, not because of a lack of love, but because my parents had had no model for this kind of emotional expression. Then too, mom was probably too drained by her 14-16 hour working days to have energy for playing with a young child. But although she could not express affection openly, my mother revealed her unspoken love for her husband and children through her cooking and house-keeping, her music, and her calm affirmative speech, and was loved and respected by us in return.

Vegetation

Dad had planted trees in two groves, one on the West, the other on the North to stave off the freezing winds around the new house. These trees had grown to maturity and were lovely. In the early thirties, they were still there but by the mid-thirties, because of lack of moisture and drying winds, they began to die off and soon were completely gone. Only one apple tree remained in back of our house near the cesspool, which is probably what kept it alive. There was no garden, as we had no way of watering it. For the same reason, we never had flowers. Later, two six-foot trees were planted in the yard. They didn't die but neither did they grow. They, like the family, merely existed.

Wayward Winds of the '30s
In Loving Memory

Of my brave and stalwart father who
affectionately called me "Girly."

Of my dear, steadfast mother who lived
vicariously through me—loving my voice recitals,
acting in plays and various other activities,
but whose proudest moment was my
graduation from Augustana College in 1949.

Lorraine Asper in Voice Recital

Lorraine Asper, senior from Artesian, presented her senior voice recital last night in Augustana's Old Main chapel. Miss Asper, a soprano, was accompanied by Audrey Fossum, senior from Canton.

A member and soloist with the a capella choir, Miss Asper starred in the campus musical, "A Little Learning." Playing a straight dramatic role, she portrayed the feminine lead in Augustana's production of "The Man Who Came to Dinner."

Newspaper clipping
Spring 1949

Bibelen

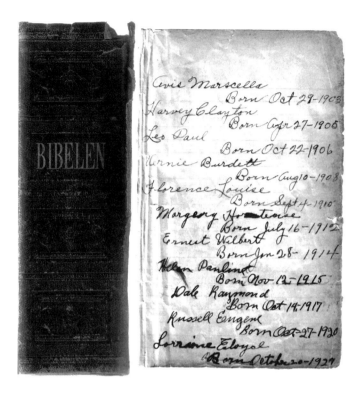

This list of Hans and Milda's eleven children was found in dad's family Bible. At over one hundred years old, it is shaped very different from the modern day Bibles, measuring 6" width by 9" length by 3" depth. This "Bibelen" is written in Norwegian. Milda had one just like it. These Bibles were their confirmation gifts.

When young Lutheran boys and girls reach the age of twelve, they begin their religious training. This takes two years of study. When their course of study is completed, the group stands before the congregation. The pastor tests them on what they have learned from the catechism. After the group has answered the questions satisfactorily, there is a confirmation service.

They then partake of their first communion, and are now full-fledged members of the Lutheran Church.

Avis Marcella Asper

Avis Marcella Asper (1903 - 1996)

Avis, my oldest sibling, and Hans and Milda Asper's first child, was born October 29, 1903, on a farm near Alcester, South Dakota. At the age of seven, Avis and her three younger brothers moved to a farm that Dad had purchased, northwest of Artesian. She attended a one-room school along with her siblings and took piano lessons from her mother who had been a piano teacher before her marriage. When Avis finished eighth grade, there was no transportation for her to attend high school. However, Mother insisted that she attend Augustana Normal School in Sioux Falls, where she took courses to become a grade school teacher. This one-year period of her life was a particularly joyful experience for Avis. She was just seventeen, away from home for the first time, and in Sioux Falls, a big city by the standards of that day. Avis loved learning and meeting new people, and she must have enjoyed being free from childcare and housekeeping.

Avis started her teaching career in 1921, teaching in various one-room country schools for the next several years. She would room and board with the parents of one of her students. Later, she taught at our home school, having her little brothers Dale and Russell as two of her students. In 1930, the school board decided to close the home school because of low attendance, and that marked the end of Avis' teaching career.

She decided she wanted to try a new field of endeavor and attended business college in Sioux Falls. She needed a job and a place to stay and was fortunate in getting employment at the home of the Borneman's. Mr. Borneman was an insurance executive and his wife served as the Matron at the police department. Mom, Dad, Russell and I stayed with the Borneman's in their very beautiful and interesting home. The oversized entrance hall featured a large stone pool with colorful fish – awe-inspiring for us country folk! The next room was all done in Chinese decor. We ate at a large, elegantly adorned table where Mrs. Borneman presided, never leaving her chair, as Avis did all the cooking and serving. This was truly a momentous episode in my young life.

Upon completion of her schooling, Avis found a bookkeeping job in Woonsocket with the Farmer's Union. She enjoyed this job very much. She boarded with the Trembly family, with whom she became fast friends, maintaining this friendship for the rest of her life. Avis attended the Lutheran church in town, sometimes playing for services.

One day, George Rubida visited the Asper farm to transact some business with the men. George had a farm near Forestburg, about seven miles away. When he first met Avis, she was carrying Baby Lorraine and George thought it was her child. When they got that fact straightened out, George and Avis

15

Avis and George Rubida
Married January 18, 1935

began to court. They were married January 18, 1935, in the rectory of the Catholic church, as Avis was not Catholic. They spent their two-day honeymoon in Mitchell, South Dakota, staying with George's brother's family. The temperature was 25 degrees below zero!

These two newlyweds were in their thirties when they started out on this new venture. The timing couldn't have been much worse, as 1935 was the very depth of the Depression. The two of them slaved away every day, attempting to eke out a living. Avis learned to milk cows which she did when George was busy in the fields. In the early spring, they would buy baby chicks to raise for eating and selling, and both cream and chickens provided a small income for them.

Part of the farm had a small creek running through it, an offshoot of the James River. The creek bed was in a small valley many feet lower than the farmland. Down there, trees and vegetation were kept alive by the running water. It was cooler too, an oasis compared to the blistering temperatures and barren foliage on the higher ground. Avis and George always planted a large garden on the flats next to the creek so there was plenty of water helping everything to grow well. Avis loved serving fresh lettuce, tomatoes, carrots and cucumbers for dinner, something we'd seldom had at home. Their garden produced so much she'd can corn, tomatoes, green beans, and more, providing an abundant supply of vegetables for the winter. There was one drawback; the garden was about a quarter mile from the house, and the gardener also had to climb up and down a steep hill.

Next came the children; Darrel Authier was born February 10, 1937. His esophagus did not lead to his stomach, so he underwent surgery on the second or third day after birth when the doctor discovered his problem. He was kept in the hospital for about three weeks. When Darrel finally

Darrel Rubida (2)

16

came home, Avis asked me to come and help take care of him, as she had to bathe him, make a special formula and give him medication everyday. He was to lie flat on his back so as not to disturb his stitches. It didn't take long for Darrel to recover fully, but taking care of his needs, along with all the other farm and housework, caused Avis a lot of stress. The next boy, Dennis Asper Rubida, arrived August 8, 1940; fortunately, he was in good health.

George was a very clever and industrious man. He decided they need a milk house so he built a small building right over the free flowing well. He made a tank of concrete that the cool water would run through, keeping the milk and cream cans cold. Since it was very close to their house, it served as a handy ice box/refrigerator. Their old farm house

Darrel (4) Dennis (1)

had very uneven floors and the kitchen was huge, making it hard to heat in winter, so George put up walls making the kitchen about half the size and much cozier. They had no bathroom so they bathed in a tin tub. Their house was heated by potbelly stoves that burned wood George cut from his grove of trees. George was the only farmer we knew in the 1930s who had a pickup truck. It was very useful for him on the farm, although not a very spacious vehicle to accommodate a family, but all four were used to being packed in on their trips into town.

Despite all the work Avis had to do, she loved to sew, quilt, embroider and crochet when she could find the time. She was an extremely good cook and enjoyed cooking. She was a great housekeeper and kept everything organized and clean. One always felt a warm welcome when entering her home. She played the piano at the Forestburg Lutheran Church for many years. She wrote letters to her siblings who were now living out of state.

Avis and George worked tremendously long hours to keep their farm going while attempting to utilize their land, cattle, and chickens to the fullest extent. By the late thirties, the dust storms had subsided and the weather patterns were changing so more rain and snow were enriching the land. The next decade would prove to be much more profitable for this couple, making their hard work more fruitful.

Home, Home on the Range

Was there any piece of equipment used more than the cook stove? This range did a myriad of tasks that touched every member of the family. It was a mass of black iron weighing hundreds of pounds. Its only decoration was the cobalt blue enamel on the oven and the warming-oven doors.

A wood box stood right next to it, stacked with corncobs and sometimes coal at the ready to satisfy the stove's ravenous appetite. The entire family kept busy feeding this monster. The older boys and Dad chopped large pieces of wood; the younger ones filled a bushel basket with cobs picked from the pigpen and others rushed down to the cellar for a scuttle of coal. The stove only rested at night.

The first person up in the morning, usually my dad, would have to stoke the embers with fuel to bring the stove back to a high heat. He'd put the teakettle to boil for the hot cereal and the coffee made from cold Artesian water.

In the dead of winter, frost formed on the insides of the windows and the upstairs bedrooms were very cold. I remember as a little girl hurrying down-stairs in my "jimmies." Dad would open the oven door to let out the heat. I'd lay my long beige cotton stockings on the door to warm while I struggled into my winter underwear. I'd fold over the bottom part of the leg and then care-fully pull on my stockings. These were attached to garters that were attached to a homemade kind of bodice. I would wiggle into my woolen skirt (No pants in those days!) and my woolen sweater. It was warm and cozy huddling next to the oven door during this rather complicated process. With only my shoes to buckle, I was then ready for a good hot breakfast.

Our range was also a water heater. Most ranges had a water tank attached on the side near the oven, but the water was only tepid. We didn't have a water tank; we had hot and cold running water! There was a large hot water tank in our bathroom. Pipes ran from the tank through the adjoining wall to the firebox in the range. Voila! Hot water! We had to be careful when we were in the bathroom not to touch this ugly metal tank as it was very hot, but it kept the room warm and cozy.

I have great admiration for my mother who knew how to handle this iron beast of a stove. She had to feed it just the right amount of fuel for each par-ticular culinary item be it an angel food cake, the daily bread, water to boil or a steak to fry. She did it by touch and feel as there was no temperature gauge. I am in awe when I think about this as I stand in my electronic kitchen with an oven that produces the exact heat I need and burners that can be adjusted instantaneously. I do believe my mother and all the women of that day were really mini-engineers controlling their wood ranges.

This stove saw constant use with our large family. As soon as breakfast was over, mom would start to make the dessert for noon dinner. She'd make two or three pies or a large cake. Then if she planned a roast, it would go into the oven in a large roasting pan. The oven was smaller than those today so a big meal required careful scheduling. Sometimes things would come out and be set aside while something else baked. Then everything would be put back in to be finished.

Mom often had a pot on the back of the stove full of skim milk. This would slowly become curds and whey and hence cottage cheese which she would serve to us or to the young turkeys and chickens. The stove also saw use for heating flat irons, making soaps, rendering lard, canning meats, fruits and vegetables, and making jams and jellies. Pans were stored in the warming oven.

Mom had few recipes and treasured new ones friends would give her. I looked forward to the big pot of navy beans with molasses and brown sugar which baked for hours. Rice was for Sunday night supper. She cooked it slowly in a double boiler and then served it with milk, cinnamon and sugar for a cereal-dessert. But for Norwegians the potato was the *staple*, and mom served potatoes with nearly every main meal, boiled, mashed or fried.

Perhaps the most memorable aspect of the old range was the wonderful aroma of freshly baked bread and cinnamon rolls which she'd make two or three times a week. That delicious smell would greet me when I'd return from country school in the late afternoon on a chilly day. I can't think of any scent that sends such a message of love and signifies the essence of home. Pillsbury got to the core of the idea with "Nothin' says lovin' like somethin' from the oven."

Christmas time was *Lefse* time! This was a formidable task for the old stove. Mother would roll out this potato dough into the thinnest large rounds you could ever imagine. She'd let no one else do this. The top of the stove was cleaned and ready. We were then allowed to roll up these large rounds of lefse on a wooden stick and then unroll them directly onto the range. The surface was quite hot so the lefse would cook quickly and not become tough. We had to keep moving it with the stick to keep it from burning. One of the older girls would be allowed to turn it to bake on the other side.

Mom would make dozens of lefse. It was a tremendous amount of work, but she loved it and I'm sure felt she was handing down a piece of her Norwegian heritage to her children. We'd slather it with homemade butter and sometimes fill it with meatballs. Or it could be a dessert sprinkled with white or brown sugar and rolled up like a cigar. What a special treat!

Cooking in our house meant preparing three big meals everyday for several children plus a hired hand or two. We were always well fed. Sitting around our large oval oak table, our family felt blessed, contented, loved and accepted while partaking of this food that had been made by loving hands. None of us were demonstrative with hugs and kisses, but my mother's love came through in her baking and good plain cooking.

The old range, too, needed some tender loving care. A couple of times a week the ashes were emptied. A small crank shook out the firebox of little leavings which would fall into the ash drawer at the bottom of the stove. The drawer slid out and the ashes were dumped outdoors. When the cook top was cold, it got some kind of polish. So, the old cook stove never required much attention and never broke down. It just did its job day after day. What a majestic piece of equipment!

Our Olson Rug

Our living room had a nicely polished wooden floor with a large rug covering the middle. Mother had saved pieces of wool for several years until she had enough to make this rug. These scraps were sent to the Olson Rug Company of Chicago. They took these scraps, dyed them and fashioned them into a very deep orange/brown 9 x 12 rug, which lasted for years. Twice a year, the men would carry the rug outdoors and hang it on the fence. We'd take turns hitting it furiously with the dust beater to rid it of six months of accumulated dirt. It was aired for the rest of the day and then repositioned on the living room floor.

Harvey Clayton Asper (1905 - 1957)

It seems there are not too many truly fine men in this world, but my oldest brother Harvey was one. As the eldest son, he was a leader in our family as well as in the community. He was an unselfish man who was always concerned about the well being of others. In appearance, he was dark and handsome and very popular with the ladies.

Harvey Clayton Asper

Harvey's early life consisted of grade school and a short period in high school at Augustana Lutheran Academy at Canton. Here he was back near his birthplace, and how happy he must have been to be there again. But with such a big family back home, and new additions still arriving periodically, his schooling was cut short. He worked on our farm, then, when the fall work was done, he'd sometimes travel south to Lincoln County to pick corn. He also worked for a while at the Moe Store there. Since Lincoln County was the place of his birth and early childhood, it had a strong place in his heart and really felt like home. While there, he enjoyed visiting his relatives including Grandpa Asper and many cousins and friends. One of his friends was Archie Gubrud who later became governor of South Dakota.

Later, Harvey delivered gasoline to farmers for the Farmer's Union at Woonsocket. In 1933, after accumulating some money, he and our neighbor's son, Art Ferguson, opened up a service station and auto repair garage in Forestburg. Harvey became a good mechanic through this experience. One night while driving to Forestburg from Huron in a Model A Ford, he evidently fell asleep at the wheel, ran into a road sign and was badly hurt. This certainly seems an unlikely accident, as the numbers of road signs in 1930 on this highway were few and far between. Harvey was taken to the Methodist Hospital in Mitchell and was in a coma for over three weeks. His left leg and hip were broken, as well as his pelvis, and he needed orthopedic surgery to insert a pin in his knee. In his wild hallucinations, he managed to almost remove this pin!

Harvey gradually improved, remaining in a private room at the hospital for several months. The family became concerned about paying the hospital and doctor bills. Our sister Helen had just graduated from high school and had no immediate plans for the future. Our parents discovered that she could work at the hospital to pay off Harvey's account, so Helen's future was quick-

Depression Family (1935)
Harvey, Ernest, Dale, Vernie, Leo, Russell, Avis, Helen, Lorraine, Mom and Dad

ly decided for her. Harvey had many friends who were also concerned about him and the great expenses he had incurred. They decided to hold a dance with all proceeds after expenses helping to pay his hospital bill. This was in the very depth of the Depression when no one had much money, so this act of generosity must have touched Harvey's heart putting his mind at ease until he was back on his feet.

Harvey came home to continue his recuperation. The folks moved out of their downstairs bedroom and Harvey took over their brass bed. This bed was never the same again as he used the brass posts of the headboard for leverage when adjusting to a more comfortable position. The posts were not up to such stress and eventually gave way, giving the bed a toothless appearance. Harvey remained in bed for several months. It was my duty to bring supplies for his morning ablution; urinal, wash bowl, cloth and towel, toothpaste and brush, and water to rinse his mouth. When he was ready for breakfast, I served him. I was only six, so felt very important and needed in this new role. Harvey would play rummy or Old Maid with me until his older brothers had time to play more adult card games. They'd play Old Maid with me, setting me up to lose, then I'd be banished to my spot beneath the table while they played!

Harvey had a huge cast on his leg for many months. It covered his left hip, leg, and foot (which itched badly). There was no physical therapy in those days. When his cast was finally removed, he first used crutches, then as his strength improved a cane. His left leg was so atrophied after all those

22

months in a cast, he had to wear a built-up shoe. His knee never bent again so he always limped, but after a number of years this became less noticeable.

When Harvey was able to walk again, he needed another, less physical, line of work. He always loved dealing with people so politics was a natural. South Dakota had a Democratic governor, but Sanborn County was always staunchly Republican. Harvey ran as the Republican candidate for Clerk of Courts against a long-time incumbent and won. Thereafter, he never had any competition for the position. This job was perfect for Harvey as he prided himself on knowing everyone in the county. Each election year it was exciting for our family to go to the rallies where a Washington representative or senator such as Karl Mundt would speak.

Harvey was a single man when he took over his new job at the county court house in Woonsocket, so he roomed in various homes. He first rented a large attic-like bedroom from Dr. and Mrs. Tchetter. They were very kind to him. One summer, the Tchetter's invited me to spend a week with them. I was in awe of this beautiful home with new overstuffed furniture, room size carpets, dining and bedroom sets, dishes that matched, a gas stove, and a refrigerator which, to my delight, held ice cream. This house was in direct contrast to ours which had always been furnished "in the need of the moment." Most impressive to a farm girl whose only experience with dogs was with large unkempt hounds who lived outdoors, was their small poodle that lived in the house!

I remember many small ways in which Harvey showed kindness to members of our family. He had acquired a Model A coupe and on Labor Day weekend, he crammed Mother and me into this tiny car to take a trip to Lincoln County. For three days we traveled between the homes of both the Asper and Hanson families. There were a lot of relatives to visit, as most like us had large families, too. Mother was so delighted after twenty years of caring for her family that she was now free to go on these yearly trips to see family and friends. She always came home with plums from which she could make her favorite tart jam.

Harvey sometimes came home for a weekend, and when I was about ten, he took me out to the pasture and taught me to drive. He was patient as I attempted to shift gears and avoid deep holes as we bounced over the rough terrain. As Mother didn't drive, this skill came in handy, as I often had to pick up my father or Leo in a distant field.

The only time I went fishing in my entire life was when Harvey took me to Twin Lakes. It was my first boat ride, too. We were out in that boat for two or three hours that felt like a lifetime to me, and all I got were three itty-bitty inedible fish. Never again! Harvey loved fishing and would go to northern Minnesota on his vacation to catch walleyed pike in those cold clear waters. I can't think of any other occasion when our staid mother was so elated as when Harvey presented her with this precious gift of delicious fresh fish, packed in ice.

Harvey didn't get married until he was forty. He enjoyed his new life as a family man with his wife Helen and their three little daughters continuing to live in Woonsocket and working as the Clerk of Courts. Sadly, he died after only twelve years of married life. Harvey belonged to the Woonsocket Lutheran Church where he always held some office. His funeral was so crowded with people coming to pay their respects that the overflow had to stand in the churchyard. Because of his open, caring, and friendly personality, he was greatly respected in his community.

A likeness of Harvey's Ford Coupe

Automobiles

We had two cars, a 1927 Chevy and a 1929 Model A Ford because we were such a large family. Leo, our in-resident mechanic, kept them running. Motors, in those days, were simple and easy to fix and maintain compared to later models. In about '39, Dad had to replace one of our old cars with a well-used '37 two-door Plymouth which reluctantly managed to get us through the next few years.

None of the six boys had a car until long after they left home and had worked hard and long to be able to afford one. I remember Harvey's first car, a two-door Ford Coupe which was very small, especially if three people rode in it. His next car was a V8 two-door Ford. When I was only 10, he'd come home for the weekend, take me out hunting and let me drive in the open pasture. This was good practice since at 11, I'd have to drive our car on narrow country roads between deep ditches in order to pick up Leo who had taken farm machinery to a distant field and needed a ride home. I could barely see out of the windshield. Having to shift sticky gears while managing the clutch was a very scary situation.

Dale and Russ didn't have a car until after WW II. When someone got a new car, everyone would rush out to inspect that particular model. And would you believe? You didn't have to have a driver's license in those days!

Leo Paul Asper

Leo Paul Asper, The Quiet Man (1906 - 1969)

My brother Leo had good reason to be known as the quiet Asper. He was the third child in the family with an older brother and sister who were very verbal. With other siblings following closely behind him, he just let others do the talking and he remained soft spoken all his life. In his formative years, Leo was exposed to two languages, with Norwegian being the primary one. When he was about four, the family moved from the close-knit Norwegian community in southeastern South Dakota, where he was born, in Sanborn County near the town of Artesian. English would eventually be the only language spoken in his home, as there were few Norwegians with whom to communicate in this new environment.

Leo's early education took place at the home school just a mile away from our farm. He and his siblings walked to school, each carrying their lunch in a syrup bucket. If the weather was terribly cold, dad would drive them in a wagon or sleigh and during blizzards, they stayed home. Leo attended school for eight years, learning the fundamentals of reading, writing and arithmetic. He did attend Augustana Academy in Canton for a short period of time and was disappointed he couldn't continue. In this time period, it wasn't unusual for twelve-year-old boys to end their formal education and start their on-the-job training, as it took many hands to keep a farm functioning.

Sometime after World War I, dad bought the family's first car and tractor. Leo taught himself mechanics and became extremely proficient at repairing machinery. No one was ever called in to fix anything on our farm, as Leo was the master mechanic. Leo no doubt felt great pleasure after solving an especially difficult mechanical problem, but he probably got little praise for it as dad just expected it of him. Being a mechanic is solitary work, so this fit with Leo's quiet personality. As the popularity of motorized vehicles grew, mechanics were needed to repair them, so Leo was in on the ground floor of this trend. Little did he know this would eventually become his life's work.

Entertainment for the older siblings consisted of walking to the neighbors, the McKillop's, to play bridge, a game Leo really enjoyed. Occasionally, he would attend dances at Ruskin Park where live big bands played on Thursday nights (Lawrence Welk played there early in his career). Sometimes Leo would meet his girlfriend Bernice Peterson at the park, usually accompanied by her mother. On Sundays, he would attend services at Artesian Lutheran Church where he had been confirmed. Confirmation classes must have been where he first met Bernice.

In the early 1930s, we were a two-car family. On Saturday nights, the young men took the Model A Ford and the old folks and kids piled into the 1927 Chevrolet for the Saturday night journey into Artesian. By the mid-thirties, we were down to only our well-worn Chevy, so Leo had no car. On

Saturday and Wednesday nights we'd go to town, dropping Leo at the Peterson home so he could see Bernice. When it was time to go home, we'd pick Leo up. I would strain to see them kissing goodnight in the dim porch light. Bernice had a Chevrolet Coupe, so Leo finally got a car when he and Bernice wed.

Leo loved pheasant hunting and was an excellent shot. Mother wanted pheasant killed only by Leo as he hit the birds in the head so no shot had to be taken out of the flesh. Leo often took uninitiated hunters out and taught them the art of hunting. He saw to it that no one ever went home without their daily limit of birds. Fine restaurants serve pheasant under glass as an exotic dish, but in our Depression-era home, pheasant was a staple at our table in the fall!

By the mid-thirties, hard times were getting worse and many of Leo's siblings had left home, either to get married or to find jobs in other towns or states. His younger brothers, Dale and Russell, were living in Artesian, attending high school and working. Leo ended up the only one at home to help dad farm. They struck a bargain that they would farm together with Leo getting a percentage of the profit at harvest time. Unfortunately, because of the drought, the dirt storms, and the rains coming at the wrong time, there were almost no crops for them to harvest, so there wasn't much money to divide.

Leo stayed on the farm until the late 1930s. His brother Vernie was living in Artesian running a gas station and garage for car repairs. He asked Leo to work for him as a mechanic and he accepted. Leo was no doubt ready to start

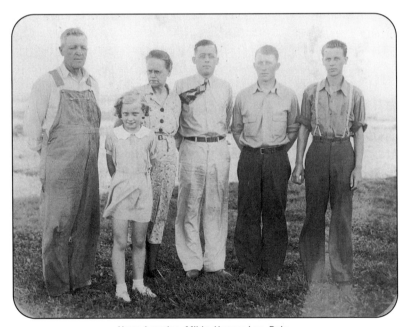

Hans, Lorraine, Milda, Harvey, Leo, Dale

28

on a new way of life after his experiences with farming. In addition, he was in his early thirties and probably felt it time to be breaking away from home. Vernie was an outgoing entrepreneur and Leo was a quiet technician; their complementary personalities made the business a success. When Vernie began selling International Harvester Company equipment the business branched out into repairing farm machinery, a job at which Leo was well experienced.

Leo was a kind and well-liked man. He was respected throughout the surrounding area as a most competent serviceman. After a very long courtship, Leo and Bernice were married in June 1940, in a small ceremony at the Lutheran parsonage. They started out on their new lives by settling into a cute one-bedroom house with their Chevy Coupe parked in their tiny garage.

Dumbwaiter

In the sweltering summertime, we used our dumb waiter to keep food cool, not cold! This contraption was built right into the cupboard wall, making it appear as though it was just another compartment. Food that could spoil easily, like butter and cream, would be set on shelves; the "waiter" would be lowered by ropes to the basement, where the temperatures would be a few degrees cooler than at ground level. In 1913, when it came on the market and when the house was built, this was, no doubt, a very innovative invention.

Leo, The Thresher

Leo had status in our community because he owned a threshing machine. About mid-summer, he would go to the neighboring farms and see if he could get five or six farmers who wanted their grain thrashed to sign on and to be part of the crew. There were always three or four Leo could count on, and there was one who wavered each year as to which threshing crew he would join. Leo would come home angry, feeling this neighbor was playing hard to get and demanding special concessions. Once the threshing crew was complete, Leo would make a roster detailing each farmer's numerical position and their approximate starting date.

Threshing time was exciting for everyone. It was a break from their usual routine. The woman of the house had to plan menus and triple their recipes to make huge quantities of food for the men. As their work was so strenuous, the workers needed many calories for energy. The lady of the house would find another woman to help her, as she not only had to cook and serve a huge dinner, but also a mid-morning and a mid-afternoon lunch with plenty of coffee. Despite the hard work involved, this event was a social time. The men didn't get together often as most weren't very neighborly. Since some were first generation, they still carried their immigrant mind set. This was true of Hans and Milda who were Norwegians clinging to their old ways, plus they were staunch Lutherans while none of their neighbors were. So they too weren't able to readily accept or give friendship easily. It would take another generation or two for the neighborhood to be truly acculturated Americans.

But much work had gone on before threshing time. That was harvest time where a machine called a binder would cut and bind the grain in the field into small bundles. Then a field hand would walk into the field, pick up several of these bundles leaning them upright against one another to make a shock. Over a period of time, the grain bundles dried out making them ready for threshing. If it should rain during this time, the worker would return to the fields turning the bundles so they would dry out and not rot. This was a cruel trick of nature during the 30s – it wouldn't rain when it was desperately needed while the grain was in the field, but would rain during the harvest or threshing time making twice the amount of work for the farmer!

Leo had many responsibilities as the owner of the threshing equipment. His tractor was a Case; heavy-duty wheels with steel rimmed lugs. He would have to see that the tractor was in good repair, as it had to run all day, furnishing power to the threshing machine. Since the threshing machine was only used one season a year, it had to be inspected carefully. It stood outside, so the weather would rust and batter it badly. It was imperative that none of the equipment break down on any day, leaving a group of idle men standing around thinking of all the tasks waiting to be done on their own farms.

Each crewmember would arrive in a hayrack pulled by horses. There would be approximately six hayracks that picked up bundles in the field. Two would be on either side of the machine feeding the bundles into the trough, then they would hurry back for more bundles while two more racks took their place – a production line. The men worked hard and steady. This was August, the hottest part of summer. The men all wore straw hats, long sleeved chambray shirts to protect their arms from the chaff. They'd carry a big red handkerchief to wipe their sweaty faces, and wore strong high top work shoes to walk on the uneven stubble.

The crew had been in the field since very early, so at about ten o'clock, a huge pot of coffee and sandwiches would arrive. The crew took a brief break to replenish their depleted energy – then back to the fields.

At dinnertime, the men would come up to the farmhouse. They washed their hands and grimy, sweat-flushed faces on a make shift wash place outside the house. Then they'd go inside, gather around a greatly enlarged table and scarf down mountains of food – lots of meat, potatoes and bread. They drank copious amounts of fluids then cake or pies for dessert. After a short rest period, they'd return to the fields hoping to finish up this job by day's end. Then on to the next farm until they all had their grain threshed.

The farmer would have to decide where they wanted their straw stacks located, so Leo would know where to set up the threshing machine and tractor. Each farmer would bring one or two extra men, as there were many tasks to do. On the day that threshing finally started, Leo would pull his thresher out to the field and place it in the assigned position. He turned the tractor around facing the thresher. Then he took a wide leather belt placing it on the thresher's flywheel, then twisted the belt once, placing the other end on the tractor's power wheel. Leo then backed up the tractor so the belt had just the right tautness. This was the power source for separating the grain from the chaff. Then everyone would take their place in the production line, some picking up the grain bundles in the field, others pitching them into the feeder trough.

A wagon or a truck would be backed up to where the grain spewed out. Here there was a hopper scale that weighed the grain so Leo would have an accurate accounting of each farmer's grain. It was Dale and Russ' job to keep the grain evenly distributed in the grain box.

At the end of the process, the wagon or truck that caught the grain would bring it to the elevator in town. Here the grain was weighed, tested for quality and stored. The farmer would be paid. Leo would then collect his share on the number of bushels from each farmer's harvest. Threshing was an important part of Leo's income during these years.

On one hand, these farmers undoubtedly enjoyed a mutual feeling of satisfaction as the season's crop was successfully harvested. On the other hand, these Depression farmers, after months of hard work and worry, sadly realized their harvest returns didn't even pay for the seed that had been sown in the spring!

Dirty Thirties

How can one describe the horrors of the "Dirty Thirties"? I remember as a young child beholding these storms that came several times a year, from spring to fall, during the early and mid-thirties. All of a sudden, about mid-afternoon, the sky would darken and the wind would start to pick up. This was an omen that one of those rolling dirt storms was on its way and would arrive in less than an hour. This meant that everyone was alerted to start preparing to batten down the hatches, to get everything prepared for the coming onslaught.

The men in the field would finish cultivating one more row before they needed to start for home (often reluctantly since this field would have been completed by day's end) whether they were driving horses or tractors. If horses, they hurriedly got them into the barn removing their harnesses. Then the men would fasten all the barn and shed doors securely, and if time permitted, help the women folk get the chickens into their coops and close those doors. "Turkey," as it is used in our modern vernacular, is so absolutely an appropriate word as there is nothing more stupid than turkeys. We would attempt to chase them straight into their abode and they'd veer off to the right or the left. Because they were frightened, they became skittish, extending their long necks high which swayed back and forth as they ran clumsily, lifting their legs so high, they must extend their wings for balance. This was a most hilarious sight but not a laughing matter at this stressful moment! Meanwhile, you were under duress and losing complete control until you had two or three helpers to herd these stupid gobble-de-gooks into their lair.

Then everybody raced toward the house while looking to the west to watch this frightening spectacle approaching. The sky had become completely black shutting out the afternoon sun. The black rolling dirt was being pushed by high winds. One could feel the pressure of the wind preceding the dirt and making the tumbleweeds roll at a fast clip stopping only when they hit the fence then piling themselves the height of the fence. A drop of rain falls and we rushed into the house slamming the door tightly shut to keep out this foreboding menace. Everyone was very tense and orders were shouted out, "Shut the upstairs windows! Get the clothes off the line! Close the parlor and dining room windows and doors! Leave a window open a crack to equalize the indoor and outdoor pressure!" This kind of pressure had sucked out our bay window before.

Now we were all milling around restlessly waiting for the full impact of the storm to hit. Then we could hear and feel the force of the sand and grit hitting the house with such might, we could only pray the roof would stay on. Suddenly, fierce lighting would fill the sky, striking close to our house followed so quickly by earsplitting thunder, we would quake with fear. These fantastical electric storms could last up to a half-hour or more, but seemed like an eternity to us. Then the rain would come in great deluges hitting the parched earth that was so dry and so packed it could not at first absorb the water. Puddles would stand around for hours after the storm. How I loved to run through those puddles in my bare feet, squishing the muddy water between my toes, flitting from puddle to puddle, sitting and rolling in the mud. What a happy experience that was for me and what a contrast to the tempest we had just encountered!

However, the adults had other more serious thoughts to consider – were the house and outbuildings damaged? How have the crops withstood this storm? Or, if harvest time, how soon do we have to go out to turn the grain shocks so they'll be completely dry for threshing? Then the rest of the day was a kind of holiday as no more work could be done – too early for chores – too wet to slop around outdoors. So, mom would put on the coffee pot to stabilize the shaken nervous systems with perhaps a little cake or some cookies, as one never just had coffee in a Norwegian home!

The result of the storm would be that it literally dumped dirt into every part of our house. Even though the house was tightly closed, grit would filter in around the windows and doors which made it feel and sound like we were walking on sand. An immediate general house cleaning was in order as one could not even eat at the dusty table or on the grit-laden dishes until all were washed. So this is one example of how that abhorrent name, Dirty Thirties, came into being.

Of course the wind blew much of the time on the plains and with it, dust and the Russian thistles which would be stacked higher than the barbed-wire fence. When times became destitute for feed, the cattle would be fed the thistles! I can still remember the sound of the wind as it would creep in around the crevices of the kitchen door – a high-pitched drone or sometimes a low moan. This wind could last for days at a time. One was housebound and felt edgy, lonely, bored and trapped. It was said these unrelentless winds drove many a prairie housewife mad! Whenever I have since been in places where there are persistent winds, I feel a great loathing come over me, reminding me of those unendurable days of listening to those eerie prairie winds.

Farmers lost their land in two ways: first, because the topsoil had blown away and secondly, since they could raise no crops in this dry windy prairie, the bank foreclosed. The lifeblood had been sucked out of the soil as well as the people who tilled it. It was the end of an era for the mid-western American farmer.

Vernie Burdette Asper (1908 - 1992)

When the stock market crashed in 1929 and the Great Depression began, Vernie had just turned 21. At the time there were not many prospects for a young man attempting to get a start in life. Vernie was still living at home, trying to find himself in a large, busy household and attempting to find work away from the farm as he and Dad did not get along very well.

It seemed that Dad was continually finding fault with Vernie. Vernie had a mischievous nature, and when in his teens, he found it difficult to live up to Dad's expectations, he became rebellious. When tensions ran high, he and Dad would get physical. Dad was very

Vernie and Ruth
Married December 25, 1936

strict and perhaps used too much discipline. But he must have felt a great sense of responsibility trying to bring up six sons to be responsible, honest, hard-working, church-going, non-drinking exemplary citizens and a credit to the Asper name. Hans's total training for fatherhood came from his own strict upbringing, during which the prevailing philosophy was "spare not the rod!" Certainly Vernie was a fun loving young man and more than ready to go out into the world and be on his own!

For a time, he and his brother Leo participated in a Works Progress Administration (WPA) project, fixing nearby country roads. They each made $2.50 a day and the horses and wagon earned an extra $1.00. Of course, this work had to be done after harvest time and before the heavy snows of winter set in, so their earning power was curtailed by the weather. I remember seeing my brothers in layers of their warmest clothes topped with heavy sheepskin-lined coats, caps with ear flaps, and perhaps a scarf wrapped around their necks and faces to protect them in the below-freezing weather. They carried lunch pails with cold sandwiches and a thermos full of hot coffee. They'd come home by late afternoon, nearly frozen and anxious for a hot supper. It was a depressing job and paid little for their efforts and bodily discomfort. Vernie only had an eighth-grade education. Traveling the six miles to attend high school in Artesian was not an option as it had also not been for his three older siblings. In his teens, he was sent for a quarter-term to Augustana Academy in Canton where he was able to play football. This was the highlight of his young life. One of his friends and fellow football players, Archie Gubred, in later life became governor of South Dakota. Vernie and Archie kept in contact through the years. All his life, Vernie regretted his lack of education. How proud he must have been in later life when his three children obtained their college degrees!

In about 1933 or 1934, Vernie moved into Artesian to work at Rapp's gas station. He found room and board with the Brice Hines family. No doubt he relished this new life away from home and started getting ideas about going into business on his own. The only two gas stations in town were located across the highway from one another, each hoping to get some highway business in addition to the local trade. In about 1936, Vernie opened a station two blocks south on main street with the plan of catching the trade of farm folks coming into town from that direction. He was quite successful and later opened a garage in his station for repair work on cars.

The Artesian School Board announced they needed a school bus and people could submit bids. Vernie's bid was accepted, so he bought a truck chassis and had a small plywood house built on the back. Inside this house, long planks were fastened down each side and a shorter one across the back. These would be the students' seats. There were windows along the sides and one in back. On the right side of this boxy contraption, a doorframe was cut at an angle and a door was installed that could be opened by a lever the driver manipulated from the front. This box-like affair's orange paint job was about the only resemblance it had to a real school bus. It had no heat to counteract the freezing temperatures present for most of the school year. No thought was given to any kind of safety measures. There were no complaints from the parents of these high school students, however, as they were overjoyed to have a

Audrey, Vernie, Lorraine, Mom and Dad

way of transporting their children to school. Ironically, transportation had been the thing that kept Vernie from higher education and now he was providing it for other farm children. He hired Eugene Anderson as the bus driver, who also worked for him at the station when he was not transporting students. Counting the filling station and repair garage, this was Vernie's third business.

Vernie had been courting Ruth Thompson for some time. She had a two-year teaching degree from Dakota Wesyelan in Mitchell and taught first and second grade in Artesian. Vernie and Ruth were married on Christmas Day, 1936, at the Lutheran Parsonage by Pastor Johnson. After the ceremony, Ruth's parents Bill and Amy Thompson hosted a lovely dinner at their home. The newlyweds kept the news of their marriage quiet, as married women were not allowed to work in the school system.

Audrey and Dad, Vernie

Perhaps the School Board's reasoning was that married women might get pregnant and it was society's duty to shield innocent children from such an intimate event. In addition, there were so few jobs during the Depression that family men came first when hiring. Ruth only wanted to finish out the year and resigned in May. Ruth helped Vernie with his company's bookkeeping until their first child, Audrey, was born September 1, 1939, when she became a full-time mother. Their first home had been in an apartment in the Thompson's house. In 1938, they moved into the Artesian parsonage, a two-story house, including a basement with a large coal furnace, four bedrooms and one bath, all for only $8.00 a month.

In the late 1930s, South Dakota began recovering from the drought and farming got back into full swing. After ten years of hard times, the U.S. economy started recovering from the Great Depression. The country was now slowly moving forward; there were jobs available and the future looked bright. Vernie was approached by the International Harvest Company with an offer to go into business with them selling farm machinery. It was a good time to be in that business, as most farmers hadn't bought machinery in years. Vernie accepted International Harvester's offer and started his new business by attaching a corrugated building behind his gas station/garage. He displayed new equipment in this space, placing large machines outside. It is said that location and timing are the keys to success in starting a new business, and Vernie had both. Conditions for growing crops were great now with plenty of rain keeping the soil in place, so farmers harvested bumper crops. With all this new-earned money and the need for new modern machinery, Vernie had an ideal business situation. Artesian was the largest town in a wide area so Vernie's location proved to be ideal. Also helping his businesses was the loyalty of farm people who endeavored to support their local merchants. Everyone in these small communities recognized that they needed each other to survive.

With the help of these favorable conditions, Vernie's ventures grew steadily. His brother Leo came to work for him as an expert mechanic, fixing both cars and farm machinery. Vernie was now a successful and well-liked merchant in the community. He was eventually elected mayor of Artesian and became a member of the School Board. World War II brought him more opportunities and challenges, as his farm machinery business helped farmers grow food for our country's troops and for our European allies as well. It had taken Vernie about fifteen years to change from a recalcitrant young man to one of Artesian's leading citizens.

PROGRAM
—

by Pupils of Ruth Thompson.

Thursday, December 28, 1933.

—

"Visit to Grandma's" ____ ____
____ ____ __ Justine Quinn
"My Poor Thumb" Randall Fisher
"Vanity of Wealth"__   "
"Rainy Day"____ Barbara Nelson
"My Stomach" __ __ Gordon Hoy
"Dorothy's Mustn'ts"_ Elsie Gere
"Who's Afraid"____ Joyce Satter
Vocal Solo ___ Delayne Anderson

PLAY
"Peddler Man"

Peddler Man ____ Harlan Fisher
Jennie __ __ __ __ Justine Quinn
Nina __ __ __ __ __ Lila Chamley
Margaret __ __ __ Lorraine Asper
Michael__ __ ___ Randall Fisher
Other village children.

—

"Punished"__ __ __ Glyde Witzel
"Mother Entertains" __ __ __
__ __ __ ___ Lorraine Asper
"Hey, Ma!" __ __ Harlyn Fisher
"Washing Dishes" Lila Chamley
Piano Solo __ __ Bernice Peterson

PLAY
"Mice Will Play"

Father Mouse__ ___ Gordon Hoy
Mother Mouse___ Barbara Nelson
(Their children)
Skip__ __ __ __ _ Elsie Gere
Skrap __ __ __ Glyde Witzel
Tiny __ __ __ __ Joyce Satter
Grimalkin, deadly enemy __ __
____ ____ ____ Randall Fisher

—

"Goodbye" __ ___ Lorraine Asper

Ruth Thompson Asper
Teacher of Elocution
WPA Project

Hi Ho the Dairy O!

It's amazing how many milk products were used daily on our farm. But along with all these good dairy products came a vast amount of work.

Milking cows was a twice-a-day chore. The milker had to get up earlier than all the other workers and complete the job before he went into the fields. Then in the evening, after a hard day's work, he had to walk out to the pasture, herd the cows home and into the barn and into their stanchions, clean their udders and finally milk them.

In the summer time, this job could be very pleasant. The barn doors were left open and there were long hours of daylight. But in winter, when it was dark and often bitter cold both morning and night, the doors were closed and only a dim lantern lit the vast cold cavern of the milking room. However, Russ, my youngest brother, says he liked the coziness of our barn in winter.

At our farm, men did the milking. Since the sexes were evenly divided, the men did "outside" chores and the women did those related to the household. But milking fit into both and many farmwomen did much of the milking. When Avis married George and moved to his farm, she learned to milk. She did it mainly during the high seasons of planting and harvesting when George was the busiest.

Two large well-scrubbed metal pails would be taken down to the barn and hung on a high hook. The cows, knowing their milking spaces, were easily led into the stanchions where their necks would be securely fastened. If the cow were a kicker, she would have her hind legs, as well as her long tail hairs, placed in leg-locks. This kept her from swatting the milker in the face with her heavy tail. This was especially important during the fly season!

The milker would take a small pail between his knees, sit on a one-legged stool and milk that "Bossy." The first drop of milk hit the empty pail with a resounding "SPLAT, SPLAT" until there was enough liquid in the bottom to silence that first explosive clatter. When the cats heard that first splat, they'd line up behind the cow and the milker would aim a squirt directly into their mouths. When they'd had enough, they'd scamper away. Some farmers named their milk cows, but our men would have considered that foolish!

When the milker finished, he would empty his small pail into the large bucket safely hanging high to keep it from tipping. There would be no crying over spilt milk! When all the cows were milked, they were let loose and sent back to the pasture. The milking finished, the large buckets were taken to the back porch of the house to the cream separator.

This separator had a very large metal vat sitting on top. The milk was poured into this vat and the crank turned to get the machine moving. The centrifugal force sent the milk swirling through 45 discs which separated the cream from the milk. The cream flowed out one spout into a stone crock and the milk streamed out a second spout into a large bucket.

Next, this separator had to be washed. At night it would be rinsed with cold water and, after it was used again in the morning, it was thoroughly washed with soapy water, rinsed with boiling water and all parts, including the 45 discs individually dried! Just another "small" task added to the housewife's busy day.

The storage of the milk and cream depended on the weather. In the summer, it was kept in our deep cave right out our back door. During the rest of the year, it would keep fine on the back porch convenient to the kitchen as it was used all day long.

We drank milk at all meals. Cream was used in coffee, sauces and whipped for desserts. Sour cream was used on breakfast toast accompanied by tart plum jam, a family favorite. Butter was used with every meal and in cooking. A pan of milk would be set back on the cook stove until it turned into cottage cheese for the family and for baby chicks and turkeys. Mother extended vegetables by creaming them; calves were weaned on the milk and what remained would go into mash for the hogs. There was no waste.

Churning cream into butter was another time consuming chore. We had a large blue square-shaped drum that fit into a metal framework to hold the drum steady and hooked the wooden paddles into place. The cream was poured into the drum, the cover replaced. Then the crank was turned and the wooden paddles beat the cream into butter. When the crank would turn no more, we had butter. It was ladled into a large wooden bowl and one of the women used a wide wooden paddle to work the excess water from the butter. This completed, salt was added and the butter placed in a stone crock.

What remained in the drum was buttermilk and this, too, was poured into jars and crocks. Buttermilk could be drunk, used in baking and was especially good in pancakes acting as a natural leavening. Mother sold buttermilk to our doctor who would often make a special trip out to the farm on the day we completed churning. All of these dairy products would be used in cakes, pies, cookies, gravies, sauces and bread.

The creamery would get the remaining cream which we'd take to town on Saturday night. It was measured for its butter content which determined its price. The cream check, along with the egg check, would hopefully pay for the family groceries for the next week.

Our parents knew that milk was good and healthy for the family and used it to the maximum. But if they'd known then what we know now about the benefits of dairy products: how milk makes strong bones and teeth, glossy hair and skin and, especially, how it acts as a deterrent for osteoporosis! It was truly a miracle product that contributed greatly to our family's general good health.

MAP OF SOUTH DAKOTA

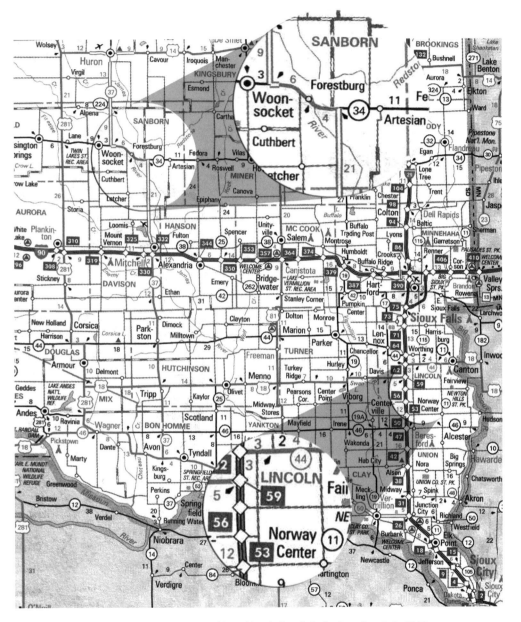

Hans and Milda Asper moved from Lincoln County to Sanborn County in 1910.

Florence Louise Asper

Florence Louise Asper (1910 -)

The year 1910 proved to be a new beginning and a great transition for the Asper family in several ways. Hans and Milda moved their family west, 130 miles away from Lincoln County where they had always lived securely surrounded by their parents, siblings, and friends. Leaving this area also meant leaving behind their familiar Norwegian Lutheran culture and exchanging rolling hills and trees for an open grassland prairie. What a shock this all must have been, but they no doubt were excited too as they now owned their own farm.

It was at this farm on September 4, 1910, that Florence Louise was born, the first Asper to be born in Sanborn County. The first Asper house had only two and a half rooms which now had to accommodate five children. Florence spent her first three years in that house, soon joined by another sister, Margery. Florence learned at an early age to help with the work of the large household, as new babies were arriving regularly. Homemaking seemed to be her calling. When she was thirteen, our neighbors, the Ferguson's, hired Florence as a general helper for $4.44 a week. She worked for them two or three summers, polishing her cooking and homemaking skills. She attended the home school for eight years until she and Margery left for high school the same year.

One day in October of her senior year, Dad asked Florence to stay home from school, as Mother was not feeling well. She was puzzled because she had never been asked to do this before, and Dr. Loring's arrival made the morning even more unusual. At about 9:30 a.m., she heard a baby's cry coming from the bedroom and she learned she had a new sister. Florence was seventeen years old and had no idea that her 49 year-old mother was expecting. That day, Florence was in charge of the kitchen and the new baby, now dressed in a dishtowel. Perhaps, still in shock, she eagerly waited for her siblings to return home from school to tell them about her exciting day.

In 1928, Florence graduated from high school – the first Asper to do so. The following week, she moved to Mitchell where she went to work at the Methodist Hospital in the kitchen, first as a cook's helper, and as she learned the trade, rising to second cook and then first cook. She was only eighteen years old and earning $80 a month along with free room and board. This was an astonishing amount of money, as even teachers weren't paid that well. She liked living in Mitchell, being on her own, and having a good job.

One event she really looked forward to was the Corn Palace festivities the last week in September. People swarmed into Mitchell to celebrate the end of the long, hard, growing season with this harvest festival. The harvest was the big pay-off time for farmers so they had money to spend. The streets were lined with carnival rides, food sellers, farm machinery and scam artists.

The main attraction was just seeing the Corn Palace itself. Each year, artists created murals made of colored corn on the outside walls. The result was truly spectacular and was about the only form of art most farmers ever saw. Inside the auditorium, a well-known orchestra and other acts would perform twice daily for five days, providing visitors with the opportunity to experience live entertainment. Mother loved this show and never failed to attend. She could not understand how most people she knew didn't attend this event. The Corn Palace still is a tourist draw, attracting even foreign visitors to the little town of Mitchell.

Florence worked for about a year and a half in Mitchell before moving to Sioux Falls, South Dakota's largest city. She worked for Barney Ordal who ran a café patronized by many of the students from nearby Augustana College. She enjoyed her work and liked Barney whose friendship she maintained through the years. It was a new experience for her to attend plays and musical events presented at the college. She roomed with an old friend from Artesian, Blanche Stekle and took her meals at Barney's. She knew she was lucky to have a good job and enjoyed buying clothes, but things were about to change with the deepening of the Depression.

Florence was a young lady who had not dated much, but in January 1933, she met Don Lukehart from Worthington, Minnesota, who had also come to the big city to work. They started to date and in May of that year, with very

Florence and Don, 1936
Gary, Don, Gloria

44

little money, they decided to elope and crossed the border into Iowa. Because of a terrible rainstorm, they couldn't get into the minister's house but he came out, got into the front seat, turned around on his knees and performed the ceremony from there. Now, that was an unusual wedding!

Their first home was with the Shegru family. They rented an upstairs apartment for $10 a month, which consisted of a living room, kitchen, and one bedroom, with a shared downstairs bath. They both worked until Florence had a baby, Don, Jr. One of the worst dust storms ever experienced in South Dakota was on the day of his birth. However, Florence was preoccupied with her caregivers who bound her up, not allowing her to walk for several days. She would not receive such care with subsequent babies. Don, Jr. was the first grandchild of the Asper family. When Florence called home to tell the news, six year-old Lorraine pleaded, "Why can't we have a baby too?"

The Depression was in full swing by this time and getting and keeping jobs was difficult. Florence had four more children in the next seven years, all born at home, Gloria in 1934, Gary in 1936, Roger in 1938 and Vivienne in 1940. Don and Florence had to hustle to feed and clothe their family. Their extended families undoubtedly wanted to help them, but everyone else was struggling as well. Fortunately, Florence was very healthy and had the same temperament as our mother. Both she and Don were hard workers. But with business so bad, they often had to accept menial jobs just to keep their family fed.

Florence and Don moved to Worthington for a while and then back to Sioux Falls. In 1938, they moved to Rochester, Minnesota, hoping there would be more jobs available in this larger, more prosperous city. Don drove a taxi, ferrying people arriving by train to visit the world-renowned Mayo Clinic. One Christmas, Mother, Leo, Avis, Russell and I drove to Rochester to visit Florence and Don. We took a ride at night to see the huge homes of the doctors. Outside, the homes were decorated with sparkling lights. We probably looked like country hicks, mouths agape at such opulence – the idea of putting lights on the outside of one's house! We were still barely eking out a living on the farm, so such decadence was beyond our imagination.

Gloria, Gary, Vivienne, Donald, Roger

Winters were long and cold in Minnesota and

Florence and Don got tired of all the heavy coats, boots, caps and mittens required for five children. They decided to try a warmer locale and thought of California, where there might be more job opportunities for their maturing clan. In August 1945, they took off for San Jose. All seven family members traveled in an old Ford, pulling a trailer behind them with all their earthly possessions.

Fortunately, California did prove to be the promised land for Florence and Don. They were able to find work and their children benefited from the availability of good high schools and affordable colleges. The Lukehart family left their Depression doldrums and entered a bright and stimulating future of opportunity.

Catalogues

What a happy day it was in the spring and fall when the catalogues, Montgomery Ward and Sears & Roebuck, would arrive by mail. It was "wish book" time. When you lived on farms near only small towns, catalogues were your major source to buy clothes. Each year, Sears & Roebuck and Montgomery Ward sent out a "Spring-Summer" and a "Fall-Winter" copy.

We'd be so excited and so eager to look at the new catalog, we'd almost fight over it. It was the most read books in our house! We "wished" we could get this dress or that coat, but mostly it was just a dream. Only underwear and other practical items would be ordered. But there were exceptions.

I remember coming home one day from country school, and there was a big package from Montgomery Ward and mom said it was for me. It was a rust-colored princess style coat that fit me perfectly. Talk about a happy girl! Amy Thompson had made my last coat from an old leftover blue coat found in her attic. She had also found a piece of fur, which she used for the collar. I had worn it proudly for a couple of years. But, oh – this new coat! It was a wish come true for a fourth grade country schoolgirl.

This is the House that Hans Built

In 1913, Hans and Milda Asper had a lovely house built for them. It was in Sanborn County, four miles west and 2 miles north of Artesian. They had six children at that time and of course not realizing their future held five more babies who would inhabit this new house.

Carpenters came from Woonsocket. Avis, our oldest sister, remembers these men sleeping in a kind of wagon with individual hutches. Mother must have fed them, and on weekends they'd return home. It took them three months to complete. It cost Hans $4,000 cash to build this house!

As a little girl this house seemed so huge to me. It was in essence only about 900 square feet on each of the two main levels. There was a full finished basement and a staircase that led to the attic which made four levels. The downstairs consisted of one bedroom, one bath, a large kitchen and dining room. From here, double folding doors led into the living room and a vestibule with a front door with an etched glass pane. This showy entrance should have been used for our guests, but most people entered by the side door directly into the kitchen.

The upstairs had a long hallway which led into the four large bedrooms. One of the boy's rooms had two beds to accommodate this vastly populated household! One bedroom had a door which opened out to the veranda.

Can you imagine how cold this house had to have been in those extremely long, cold winters on the South Dakota plains? The temperatures for months were zero degrees or less! The house had no insulation in the walls or attic whatsoever. There was a central coal-burning furnace that did the best it could with the freezing temperatures that endured all winter long. The windows in the barely heated upstairs always had heavy frost on the inside.

Our beds were covered with flannel sheets with two or more homemade quilts made of dark material. Some were pieced from old woolen clothing and were so heavy they must have weighed several pounds each. When you got into bed you couldn't move because of the weight, and you didn't move because the freezing breeze would enter your cozy cocoon.

This abode, that reared its white frame surface to the heavens, sat on the barren plains where the winds, sleet and snow whipped it in every conceivable manner. What a poor architectural creation this house was for the plains, yet was the "typical" accepted design for the majority of houses built at that time. How much better the sod shanty that preceded these homes, truly was. It stood squat with thick sod bricks which were perfect insulation against the heat, cold and unwavering winds. However, the sod house was the humble abode of the early settlers. When once the farmer had established himself on his farm, and had produced several crops, he proved his success by building a big, square two-story house that stated, "I've made it!"

However, more frugal farmers could never bring themselves to invest in a better house, but built good barns and outbuildings for they believed it was these buildings that contributed to the farm income. Their philosophy was that a barn could build a house, but a house did not build a barn. So for many farmers, their animals lived as well if not better than the families.

Hans later built a state-of-the-art large red barn. It had two long rows of stalls for the horses with a corridor running between. The cows had solid stanchions with a gutter draining to the outside. It had stairs that led to the haymow which was the size of the entire bottom floor. There were openings in the floor, so that hay could be tossed down supplying fresh hay to be distributed into the stalls downstairs. Hans built a fine house for his family and his livestock was well sheltered also.

After only ten years, Hans must have felt he was living the American Dream. Here he was, firmly ensconced on a well-provisioned farm with a large and growing family to help him in his endeavors. How fulfilled he must have felt that all his plans and hard work had turned out so well!

"America the Beautiful" extols, "the fruitful plains", but the passage of time proved this to be a fallacy. Most of the Dakota plains was marginal land. The plow should never have been put to the soil. My mother said the Norwegians, as well as other immigrants, rejoiced in coming to South Dakota as there were no trees that had to be cleared as in other eastern states. This backbreaking task could take a long time to do so the future farmer had to delay his first planting. Immediate planting was crucial, as a farmer had little income or food for his family until that first harvest. If only these budding farmers could have perceived that trees were an indication of rich soil that Dakota farmland lacked.

Because of this poor soil and the terrible winds, newspapers captioned this area the "Dust Bowl" while referring to the next ten years as "The Dirty Thirties."

MAP OF ONEIDA TOWNSHIP

ONEIDA TOWNSHIP

Scale 2 inches to 1 mile

Township 107 North, Range 60 West of the 5th P. M.

#21 – George and Avis Asper Rubida's farm

The Paradox of the Close Family

In *We Were the Mulvaneys*, author Joyce Carol Oates says "...Members of a family who've lived together in the heated intensity of family life scarcely know one another. Life is too head-on, too close-up. That was the paradox. That was the bent, perplexing thing. Exactly the opposite of what you'd expect. For of course you never give such relationships a thought, living them. To give a thought – to take thought – is a function of dissociation, distance. You can't exercise memory until you've removed yourself from memory's source."

Oates' statement could surely apply to the Asper family clan. With 24 years age difference and 11 strong – how can you really get to know someone in the hubbub of daily life that is so frantic, with so many packed bodies surrounding one? One of my sisters said she has no memory of a sister five years younger than she (two sibling in-between). I just couldn't fathom that, but perhaps other members of the family could also make a similar statement.

As Ms. Oates says, "life is too head-on, too close-up which brings on the opposite reaction one would expect." You'd think a sibling would be especially close to one of similar age, one you'd associated with since infancy. But perhaps in our family, each child was simply attempting to create his own space – his own sense of being – his own individuality amidst this swirling crush of his many siblings – a book mark between many pages and perhaps just about as impersonal.

I can see now how totally different my circumstance were and how my siblings could enjoy me, this so much younger child. It gave them the dissociation and distance they lacked with their other siblings. They each had a particular investment in me. They thought about me; each one taught me something different and through these acts possibly became more centered themselves. And the rare treat was – they could lavish hugs and kisses on me, the baby, when no other affection was shown in the family.

My family position was especially unique. I could give thought to each of them; they were all very distinct individuals to me, because I had the dissociation and distance as they were now reaching adulthood and leaving home, so by the time I reached seven, I was now the only child at home. When a sibling came home, he was the center of attention for my parents and me, but I was the center of attention for them – how much I'd grown, what new songs I knew, what was I doing at school etc. – and of course a special gift for me.

In writing these family memoirs, it has helped me understand more clearly my relationship with each of my siblings. I am truly blessed to be part of this large family as each one gave me such special consideration and loving care not only in my childhood, but throughout my life.

Margery Hortense Asper (1912 - 1994)

As the middle child between five older and five younger siblings, Margery had to fight for her place in the sun. She was bright and sassy and according to her older sister, Florence, she would sneak away when it was time to do the dishes or any other chores. Margery was never the quiet, feminine type. Tall, with a medium build and rather boyish in her looks and demeanor, she was good in sports, especially in basketball. Margery played the piano well and won typing awards for speed and accuracy. She was always quick to get her homework done and razzed those who were slower. An excellent student, she graduated from high school in 1929, in the same class as Florence.

Margery and Lloyd Cook, 1938

Our parents decided that Margery should go to Augustana Normal School in Sioux Falls for one year to obtain a teaching certificate. This amount of education was typical of most grade school teachers at that time, especially in rural areas. The pay was around $50 per month, but during the thirties when there was little money in the tax coffers, a teacher might be paid in warrants. This was not actual money, but a promise to pay when tax money became available. Sometimes Margery would have to wait for quite some time to receive her pay. In addition, as Margery lived at home, she often had to give her paycheck to dad to help make ends meet on the farm which didn't always please her.

Margery first taught at the Schaffer School, about two and a half miles from home. We drove together to school, as she was my teacher for my first two years. Like other country schoolteachers, Margery was expected to do a lot of work in addition to teaching. She had to clean the classroom, cloakrooms, entryway, basement and the outside toilet before school opened in the fall. The furnace had to be started early each winter morning so the large schoolroom would be somewhat warm when the students arrived. One year the government began a WPA program to ensure that all school children had one good hot meal a day, so cooking lunch became another duty for Margery! I can remember a large pot of potato soup heating on the kerosene stove all morning in order to be ready by lunchtime. I don't believe this project lasted very long, at least not at our school.

Of course, teaching in a country school also involved preparing for more than a dozen classes each day. South Dakota's "Course of Study" outlined

51

very specifically everything that had to be taught from first through eighth grade. It was a great help for isolated prairie teachers and provided a solid education for the student. Each year, Margery would have to organize the study program based not only on the Course of Study, but also on how many students were in each grade. For example, when I was a student at Schaffer School, first and second grade classes were taught individually, and third through eighth grades had separate math and reading classes. However, social studies and science would be taught every other year so two classes could be taught together, i.e., the third and fourth graders would have history one year and science the next. This eliminated three classes each day, making the teacher's schedule easier.

Another extra job for the teacher was supervising the Young Citizens League, or YCL. This club taught students to be aware of societal needs and encouraged good citizenship. On Friday afternoons, just before school was let out for the weekend, a short YCL meeting would be held and the students assigned clean-up jobs around the school as an exercise in good citizenship. This would be about the only help Margery had for her janitorial duties.

Of course, Margery also had to prepare the students for the Christmas program. This was a very exciting time for all the pupils. There would be parts to learn for skits, recitations and Christmas music to rehearse. The school board bought a tall tree and we all helped decorate it. Lamps would be brought to light the schoolroom as the program was always held in the evening. Coming to school at night with our parents made us so excited and awe-filled we were practically speechless. After the program, presents were handed out and each child received a bag of candy. For many children during the Depression, this might be the only present they received. Our family had the added benefit of being related to the teacher, so we got to take the huge

Christmas tree home for our celebration. Many families could not afford a tree, and once Margery stopped teaching at this school, mother would buy a small tree that never cost more than $.50.

With all these varied tasks to perform, one can see what an enormous job it was to teach in a country school. Margery was extremely organized and managed her job very efficiently. She was well liked by her students and greatly appreciated by their parents. To this day, when I return to South Dakota, I'll

Five Asper Sisters
Front: Lorraine, Helen
Back: Florence, Avis, Margery

often meet a former student of Margery's, who praised her teaching and recalled how much they liked her.

After teaching four years at the Schaffer School, Margery was ready for a change and eager to move away from home. It was decided that several of us should stay in town. Vernie, Margery, Dale, Russell and I stayed at the Cook's home in Artesian. Dale and Russell attended high school and had part-time jobs. Vernie was already working at a gas station in town. Margery started teaching at the Hanson School south of town and I started third grade in Artesian.

Margery was expected to take the place of our mother in town. She had to cook the evening meal for all of the Cooks and us after getting home from school. Our parents sent meat, eggs, milk and bread to help with expenses, but Margery's cooking never tasted exactly like Mom's. Another of Margery's duties was nurtur-

Graduation
Augustana Normal School 1930

ing her homesick eight year-old sister. Neither Margery nor I was happy with this living arrangement, and fortunately, it only lasted one year. The following school year, Dale and Russell took advantage of a new WPA program and moved into a dormitory in town. I moved back home to attend our newly reopened home school. Margery moved out to the country to teach at the Hanson School where she lived with the Hanson family and taught for four years.

She had been dating Lloyd Cook for quite some time. Dad did not like this relationship as Lloyd drank which dad was very much against. When Margery came home on weekends, dad would get on her case. At the end of the 1938 school year, they really had it out. Dad told Margery to pack her things and leave the house. His parting shot was, "Did you get everything?" This phrase must have haunted her, as she brought it up many times throughout her life. Perhaps Margery didn't have as tough a heart as she pretended to have.

Sometime earlier, Lloyd had left Artesian and had gone to Butte, Montana, to find work. He found a job so when Margery left home, she traveled to Butte where they were married June 16, 1938. Margery wanted to try a different line of work so she and Lloyd both worked in a restaurant. Marge proved to be very adept at this new job. Her life was now completely changed – new state, new job and a new marriage. These changes reflected in her personality as she learned how to enjoy her new life to the fullest.

Ernest Wilbert Asper (1914 - 1960)

Ernest was about to start his adult life with graduation from high school in 1932, at the depth of the Depression. He wasn't the greatest student, but was well liked by his classmates. He was a star tackle on the football team, had the lead in both the junior and senior class plays, and his good looks were much admired by the girls. Like many of the boys at that time, he dreamed of becoming a professional baseball pitcher and would have his siblings out in the barnyard trying to catch his fastball.

Ernest Wilbert Asper

Somehow he managed to squeeze football practice in after school before returning home with the rest of his siblings in the family car. After a busy day at school and football practice, he was still expected to fulfill his chores at home, including both the morning and evening milking. Ernest did not perform these duties stoically; in fact, he complained vociferously, but to no avail. His older brothers probably didn't feel too sorry for him, as he was the first Asper son to attend high school.

Graduation night

Ernest also complained about other things. In high school, he decided that being Norwegian was not such a good thing – perhaps his way of rebelling against the status quo. He also thought the folks didn't purchase enough magazines and other reading material for the family, although they considered themselves lucky to be able to afford a daily paper and a couple of farm journals. The older boys subscribed to the "Saturday Evening Post" and "Liberty" magazine, each five cents a copy and Ernest enjoyed reading about the exciting events going on in the outside world.

The fall after graduation, Ernest went to Lincoln County and picked corn for his Aunt Aletha and Uncle

Emil Rogness, as well as some of their neighbors. His older brothers had been doing this for several years, returning to the area where their family had started out. Though the wages were low, this seasonal labor put a bit of money in his pocket.

After bumming around for a while, including riding the rails, he joined the Civilian Conservation Corps (CCC), a program of President Roosevelt's New Deal. The CCC took unemployed young men and put them to constructive work. Ernest was sent to a camp in the Black Hills where he worked clearing woods, trimming trees and other forestry work. Because he had experience with tractors and machinery on the farm, he was chosen to be a truck driver. The CCC was loosely patterned after the military. The men lived in barracks and had regular roll call and inspections from the Army officers in charge. They received $30 per month, of which $25 was sent directly home to their parents. For these young men, ages 18 to 25, the CCC provided steady work plus room and board. At the time, jobs were almost impossible to find and even fathers would leave their families to make one less mouth to feed.

After spending a couple years with the CCC, Ernest decided to go to Michigan to look for work. An Artesian friend, Tom Wise, was working in an automobile factory there and said the pay was good. The job didn't open up immediately so Ernest worked on farms and nurseries in the area before he finally got a job in the Pontiac factory. He was now making $1.25 per hour – quite a contrast from the five dollars a month he netted with the CCC.

However, working in an automobile factory was not easy. In "Lift Up Thine Eyes," Sherwood Anderson describes the industrial tyranny that took place in these factories:

Ernest at Niagara Falls

> "In the assembling plant everyone works on the belt. This is a big steel conveyor, a kind of moving sidewalk, waist-high. It is a great river running down through the plant. Various tributary streams come into the main stream, the main belt. They bring tires; they bring headlights, horns, and bumpers for cars. They flow into the main stream. ...the assembly plant is a place of peculiar tension. You feel it when you go in. It never lets up. Men here work always on tension. There is no let-up to the tension. If you can't

stand it, get out. It is the belt. The belt is boss. It moves always forward... Not too rapidly. There are things to be done. ...They are, almost without exception, young, strong men. It is however, possible that eight hours a day in this place may be much longer than twelve or even sixteen hours in the old carelessly run plants."

While living in Michigan, Ernest lived in rooming houses or low-priced hotels, eating all his meals at cafes. Since leaving home in 1932, Ernest had nothing resembling a home life or family until he returned home in 1945 after completing his time in the Navy. What a lonely existence this must have been for him. Danny Dill and Mel Tillis write of such a life in their song "Detroit City":

> *"Home folks think I'm big in Detroit City, from the letters that I write they think I'm fine. But by day, I make the cars, By nights, I make the bars, If only they could read between the lines. I wanna go home. I wanna go home. Oh, how I wanna go home."*

On one of his trips home, Ernest had a new Buick, of which he was very proud. We all admired it, rode in it and had our pictures taken in front of it. Ernest loved clothes and was always well dressed and well groomed and probably appeared quite the bon vivant to his siblings. On another trip home, he invited his younger brother Russell to accompany him back to Michigan.

Ernest's New Buick

They stopped in Chicago, Russell's first big city, and in Detroit they saw Bob Crosby and the Bob Cats perform. Russell was duly impressed.

I remember Ernest telling me, "A man wants a happy, congenial woman, one who smiles and doesn't do a lot of complaining." That was an insightful thought for a very young girl and I'm still trying to smile more and not be critical.

Of all the siblings, perhaps Ernest was most affected by the Depression. He was on his own for a long time and could easily have become discouraged or deeply depressed. He had a mindset, however, to try anything to improve his condition, despite the defeating circumstances of the times. Perhaps some of his experiences helped prepare him for his years in the Navy as an airplane mechanic aboard the Princeton, an aircraft carrier, where he rose to be a Chief Petty Officer. Certainly, his life was varied, and although his endeavors were modest, his continual striving to better himself showed courage and great strength of character.

Home Remedies

In early farm days, one didn't rush to the doctor for every cut and mishap. One of the adults would attempt to fix the problem right then and there. For colds, Vicks Vapor Rub or Mentholatum was the favorite remedy. It would be rubbed on the throat and chest and put in the nose. These fumes gave some relief. If the cold seemed to settle in the chest, mother would make a poultice of Denver Mud. She'd take a clean cloth, apply this thick, sticky mud plaster on the cloth, warm it slightly in the oven and then apply it to the chest area. The patient, confined to his bed, would wear it for several days. This poultice drew out the infection, keeping the patient from getting pneumonia or, if he did get it, helping him recover.

For sore throats, one would apply some Vicks in the throat area and drink warm fluids. For a bad cough, mother would wrap a cold, wet cloth around the neck and give us sugar, honey or Smith Brothers Cough Drops.

Flu came every winter. Most of the family would have it at one time or another; so, this illness could last in our house for several weeks! Sore throats, headaches and aching bones kept the victim down for three or four days. Aspirin was about the only solution along with lots of liquids.

Tobacco

There were no taboos on tobacco in the thirties. No one had ever heard that it had any ill effects on the body, and it was thought to be a calming, enjoyable habit that had been practiced for centuries.

All six of my brothers smoked and my parents didn't object. My father chewed Copenhagen snuff; so, he couldn't say much to the boys. Two sisters smoked, also, but never in our parents' presence. Women in those days did not smoke openly. It was considered too racy. I remember seeing our druggist's wife smoking in the backroom of their store. I was absolutely traumatized! I told no one, but every so often that scene would play itself out in my head. It made me feel uneasy when I remembered this "sordid" scene. It wasn't until my early teens when I found out that Margery and Helen smoked and realized that they were nice people! However, as I grew up, and I saw more women smoking, I'd still feel disgust at their habit.

Since money was so scarce, the boys would roll their own cigarettes. They would buy a small, cheap cotton sack of Bull Durham. They'd need cigarette paper that came in an orange package. They'd carefully take out a thin paper wrapper, open up the drawstring tobacco sack and carefully fill the paper with just the right amount. Next, they lifted the bag upright catching the drawstring in their teeth while the right hand pulled it tight, finally placing the bag back in their shirt pocket. During this process, the left hand had to be kept level so as not to spill any of the tobacco. It was tamped to distribute it evenly, lifted to the lips, licked to wet the paper, sealed, twisted on the ends in opposite directions then lit with a big farmer's match – and smoked!

A better tobacco came in an oval shaped tin can. Prince Albert was one brand. Smart-alecky kids loved to call up the store and ask if they had Prince Albert in a can. When the answer was "Yes," they'd say, "Then you'd better let him out!"

Movies usually had the leading characters smoking. Women would have long cigarette holders which made them appear very chic.

Though ready-made packs of cigarettes such as Lucky Strike, Camels, Chesterfields or Phillip Morris cost only 15 or 20 cents a pack, they were bought for only special occasions.

Helen Pauline Asper (1915 -   )

Helen Asper Cullerton as told to Lorraine Asper Minier

Helen Pauline Asper

It was difficult being a middle child in such a large family as ours. There was so much work to be done even with many hands to help, that I learned at an early age to do what I was told to do and more. I cleaned, washed and dried dishes, set the table, hung out clothes and ironed them, and kept my clothes picked up. I also had to watch out for my younger brother, Russell. He could be quite a handful, and one day I got so frustrated with him that I locked him in the granary. Later on, when he was missed and everyone was scurrying around looking for him, I remembered where I had parked him. There were few kind words spoken to me that day!

Life on the farm was pretty routine. However, one day when I returned home from school, we had a new baby! There was great excitement over the surprise birth of this eleventh child, Lorraine. I was perhaps the only child in the family to even suspect that our 49 year-old mother had been expecting. One day I had noticed my mother carrying a clothesbasket in a way which revealed a stomach that seemed larger than usual, but being only 12 years old and not very wise in the ways of the world, I never mentioned this observation to anyone.

With the birth of Lorraine, I had a new job – caring for this five-pound infant. When I was at home, I did everything for her except the nursing: i.e. bathing, dressing, changing diapers, cuddling and cajoling her when she cried. Of course, the entire family gave the baby a lot of attention. It was amusing to see my big brothers making such a fuss over this tiny baby. There were so many arms to hold her that she hardly had time to sleep. But I was the chief nanny and I enjoyed my position feeling very grown up.

I spent my grade school days attending what we called our home school in the country. The schoolroom was usually filled with at least four Aspers, several Shefskys, and two or three stray children from other farm families. We enjoyed playing variations of tag and softball in the schoolyard when the weather was nice. In the winter, we could go down in the basement at recess and lunchtime. Of course, we each had our own lunch bucket, usually a large Karo syrup can. Some students who lived farther away would ride a horse to school. There was a barn on the school property in which to keep them.

Lorraine and Helen

In 1929, I started attending Artesian High School. I found it a nice change to meet other young people from town and surrounding farm communities. I did well in my classes, but hated algebra, probably because of Professor Fisher who taught this subject. He was so strict and exacting that his very presence made me shake. I had taken private elocution lessons which stood me in good stead when I tried out for our school theatrical productions. I won the lead in both the junior and senior plays, so those were very exciting times for me. I was also a good typist and won the bronze medal in a school-typing contest. I played first-string basketball as a guard (at that time, girls only played on a half court) and played trombone and then clarinet in the school band.

At night, I sat around our huge oak dining room table to study in the light of the Aladdin lamp with my siblings. Dad always read the daily paper then and other members of the family might gather around the light with magazines. We also enjoyed playing card games such as Some-R-Set and bridge. Every Sunday we would get dressed in our best clothes and go to church where I sang in the choir. We attended Luther League on Sunday nights. On Saturday nights, we would go into Artesian to chat with friends and perhaps enjoy a treat of candy or ice cream. Dating usually meant roller-skating or dancing at Ruskin Park. This was a large area with picnic tables, a few summer cabins, a large pavilion for Saturday and Sunday roller-skating and Thursday night dances with live bands.

After church and Sunday dinner, two or three family members might go gopher hunting. This was a pretty strenuous activity, as it involved pulling a heavy cream can filled with even heavier water in an old steel play wagon across a rocky field. When we'd spot a gopher hole, we would pour water down it and stand back, waiting for a gopher to emerge. When it did, we'd hit it with a large stick. Now the object of this violent game was not fun, but rather profit, as Sanborn County would pay us three cents apiece for each tail we brought in. Times were hard, but what a way to make a few cents!

One of the highlights of my life was getting a new dress for my prom. We went to Feinstein's, the finest dress store in Mitchell, where I picked out a long pink organdy dress. I felt like a princess and could hardly wait for prom night. When I graduated in May of 1933 with 16 classmates, my parents bought me another lovely dress.

After graduation, decisions had to be made about what I was going to do with my life. My oldest brother Harvey had badly damaged his left knee and hip in a car accident and was still in the hospital after many months. After a conversation with the hospital officials at Mitchell Methodist, my parents informed me that I could go to work there and start paying off Harvey's bill. Somehow, this didn't seem quite fair, but as it meant I would be away from home and living in a town with the opportunity to meet new people, I decided that I might like the idea.

I started work performing the most menial jobs such as loading the dish-washer, cleaning, and so on, but soon rose to working in the office, on the switchboard and other tasks. I lived right on the hospital grounds and did make new friends, even some from Artesian. We occasionally walked the mile downtown to see a movie when finances allowed. We mostly just gabbed and enjoyed being away from home and on our own for the first time.

In 1934, after being associated with nurses for some time, I decided this would be a good profession for me. Nurses' training took three years of hard work, including 32 hours of college credit. Fortunately, since becoming a nurse involved caring for patients, this on-the-job training was free. The hos-pital even paid for my uniforms, books, laundry, and room and board which was a real godsend in the middle of the Depression.

I really liked my training, except perhaps for bedpan duty! We rotated through obstetrics, surgery, the nursery and caring for patients. Our shifts were 12 hours long; on night duty we could rest for three hours on a cot in the hospital and during the day, we could rest in our rooms in the nurses' dormitory. Night duty lasted three weeks, after which we were given a short break to return home and readjust for daytime work.

The routine with patients was to bathe them, empty their bedpan, put the room in perfect order and even arrange the flowers. We were even expected to serve the food trays that arrived from the basement via dumb waiters. In our second year, we could dispense medications and record vital signs. Most hospital rooms were private. It was a very clean and well-run hospital which gave the staff a great feeling of confidence.

Helen the Nurse, 1935

Miss Mable Woods was the superintendent of the hospital. She was a tough cookie and ran that place like a general. The entire hospital staff, including the graduate nurses and maybe even the doctors, were frightened just to meet her in the hall. Her motto was: "When you're dealing with life and death, you don't go gadding about!"

Despite Miss Woods and our busy schedule, living in the dorm with girls from all over South Dakota was great fun. Our food was served in the hospital basement and was very caloric. My weight shot up to 140 pounds; after graduating and leaving the hospital, I lost twenty pounds. During our schooling, we couldn't go out on weeknights, but on the weekend, we could stay out until ten o'clock!

About halfway through my training, for no apparent reason I decided I wanted to quit. Perhaps I was just tired of the grueling routine. However, when I announced my intention at home, my mother was aghast! "What are you thinking of? What are you planning on doing?" As I could not come up with any good answer, she said, "You are going back," and that was that!

As third-year students, we added surgical nursing along with other practical training. Doctors lectured us on anatomy, psychology, medications and so on. We had very few diagnostic tools to rely on, only simple blood tests (red, white and differential) and x-rays of the 1930s variety. Tonsillectomies were common in the hospital and if a patient presented us with a bellyache, he got an appendectomy! All in all, at the culmination of all our training, we had been molded into proficient nurses.

I graduated in the summer of 1937, but had to continue to work for a while to make up for missed time. I changed my starched nurse's cap with a narrow stripe for one with a wide black stripe that signified I was a graduate nurse. I moved into an apartment with Evans and Aldrich, two of my classmates. I was offered a supervising position at the hospital for $60 a month, but decided to do private duty nursing instead. As the hospital provided no post-op nursing services, these patients usually had to hire private nurses for several days. For this type of work, I was paid $4.00 for a 12-hour day.

In 1939, Aldrich and I took a bus to Boulder, Colorado. We had sent our resumes to Boulder Community Hospital and had been offered positions. We worked there for a year and a half. We then decided to move to Fort Lauderdale, Florida, figuring that city would have a lot of old, sick, rich patients needing private duty nurses. At first we did general nursing at the hospital there, but as we got to know the doctors better, they called on us for private duty cases which were much better paying.

My sister Margery was living in Butte, Montana. In 1942, I was ready for a change, so I moved there and worked four years for Dr. Casebeer, an eye, ears, nose and throat specialist. This turned out to be a fortunate move, as it was in Butte that I met my future husband, Bob Cullerton.

Saturday Night Bath

Saturday night was the most exciting night of the week for the entire family as this was the night we all went to town! Everyone was expected to take the ritualistic Saturday night bath to get cleaned up for the trip. Then, too, we would be ready for church on Sunday morning. With only one bathroom and eight or nine people to use it, an agenda was closely followed.

Starting in mid-afternoon all systems were "go." At the top of the list was getting the bath water *running*. Our town was named Artesian because of the wells in the entire region. Our well was such a good producer that neighbors came to our place to fill their water barrels. We were lucky. Not only did we have this water supply, but also it was piped into the house having both hot and cold running water for our bath. However, this water moved mighty slowly.

We had no way of upping the pressure so getting a bathtub filled took a long time, and there were many people who would use the tub on a Saturday night. The water started dribbling into the tub in late afternoon and I was always the first one in. I could play for a long time with the water supposedly running full force, but actually trickling. After an hour there must have been only two inches of water! I'd get out and then my sisters and mother would have their turns in the same water, as we were all relatively clean.

The water continued to run so by the time my brothers and dad arrived, this well-used well water had risen to three or four inches. The men would have come in from the fields a little earlier than usual, would eat their dinner and then would take their baths. On some bad windy days, it made me laugh to see my brothers, who had worn goggles, with their round, clean eyes and mouths protruding from the black dirt clinging to their faces. They looked like a different species. But they washed all this dirt away, from their faces and from their sweating bodies and got all spiffed up to meet the hoards of people in our small town!

Our bath towels were a sorry lot. Many had no end seams. They were different lengths and colors, sizes and as thin as thin could be. I never saw a new towel come into our house during the Depression. I guess bath towels were considered a luxury for which there was no money.

After all the bathing, we followed a strict regimen. We got into our dress-up clothes, then piled into our two cars for the six-mile journey to Artesian. Room, too, had to be found in the cars for the egg crate and the can of cream we would use for trading.

Each member of the family had an agenda. One brother was dropped at his ladylove's house; another liked playing pool and probably had a beer or two, much to my father's chagrin. Mother went grocery shopping and visited with other farmers' wives. The girls went off with their friends. Dad sat outside on the street benches commiserating with his friends about the HARD TIMES. I went to the movies, the highlight of my week.

Back at the house, there was that dirty tub. No one was concerned. They were living it up in town. The next week someone would attack the rings and the dirt with a liberal sprinkling of Dutch Cleanser and a lot of elbow grease to get it shining again for the next onslaught of bathers.

Outside in the farmyard all was dark, quiet and moon lit. The windmill worked away pumping up that Artesian water as though it were almost aware of the great service it had once again rendered this Saturday night.

Clothes Washing

Monday morning everyone was on alert as this was WASH DAY! The large copper boiler, filled with water, was set upon the cook stove. While the water was heating, Mother pared a bar of P & G soap into it, stirring to melt the soap. No powdered soap was on the market, yet. When brought to a boil, the heavy pot was carried down the steep stairs to the basement and the water carefully poured into the washing machine. In the meantime, mother had sorted the clothes, whites and dishtowels to go in first, then sheets with each load graduating to the more soiled laundry, ending with overalls.

The folks bought a new Maytag washer when I was born in 1927. It was made of very sturdy, heavy metal. The motor ran on a mixture of gasoline with a small helping of oil. The first load of washed laundry went through the wringer into cold rinse water. Then the wringer was positioned so this load was wrung into a rinse with "bluing," which whitened the clothes. Finally the clothes fell into the laundry basket ready to hang on the line.

Someone would have to stagger up the steps with this heavy load, then pin the clothes on the line whether it was very windy or extremely hot. If it were freezing, the sheets would be stiff as boards when taken down, but when they warmed up in the house, they would dry and smell so fresh. This enormous job of washing would take three or four hours. Of course, life was still going on upstairs which meant someone had to be preparing a big dinner, too.

Tuesday was IRONING DAY. Monday, all clothes were sprinkled, rolled and placed in a basket so they would be evenly damp, just right for the iron the next day.

On Tuesday, two heavy flat irons were heated on the stove. When an iron grew cold, it was exchanged for the hot one. The ironer stood at the ironing board for hours at a time. Everything, but everything, had to be pressed. Well, perhaps the sheets weren't ironed. Mother used the method of washing only the bottom sheet. The top sheet was put on the bottom and a clean sheet went on top. This cut down the sheets to launder from ten to five. When the ironer was exhausted by this labor-intensive job, she'd wrap up the remaining garments, hoping to finish on Wednesday. And this was just part of the week's work.

Dale Raymond Asper

Dale Raymond Asper (1917 - 2004)

In 1930, Dale was a seventh grader at the home school with his sister Avis as his teacher. He was never very happy with school, preferring to work on his own projects. He hated reading, but liked math. Dale was practical, organized and efficient, able to size up a situation and quickly figure a way to improve upon it. This talent later proved to be a great asset in the business world.

Our local country school closed at the end of 1931, and, for a time, the four Aspers – Ernest, Helen, Dale and Russell drove to school in Artesian. During Dale's junior year, he stayed in a dorm in the Jones' home. At that time, a WPA program provided housing and meals for rural high school students so they could finish their education. The students ate all their meals in the school lunchroom with funding for the food and labor coming from the WPA. This program helped many local people: the students, their parents, the local women paid to cook and the families providing the housing. Some students wouldn't have been able to finish their education without this program as cars were few and undependable and roads, especially during the winter months, less than ideal.

Dale always worked while he was in school. His first employer was the Knutson family; he worked in their bakery and lived in their home. However, the bakery soon closed for lack of business and Dale went to work for Bill Quinn, who ran the local department store. Initially Dale was put in charge of men's clothing; later he was transferred to the grocery department. He liked his job in the grocery store and learned a lot about business. He received much praise from Mr. Quinn, something he'd never received at home. During his last year of high school, Dale worked in a drug store for John Foote, a pharmacist. Here, he continued his on-the-job management course, learning how to order goods and handle customers. These two jobs fit his talents to a T, and his self-esteem grew when both bosses showed their appreciation for his excellent work.

After graduating in May of 1935, Dale continued to work until the fall when he decided to seek his fortune out West. He hitchhiked to California where he met his Ulberg cousins, Howard and Lester, and his Rogness cousin, Enoc, near San Diego. He lived with them for a while and found a job on the assembly line at Consolidated Aircraft, making PBYs for the Navy. Dale worked there during the winters of 1936 and 1937, making 35 cents an hour, for a grand total of $56.00 a month.

When Dale was a high school senior, he had the opportunity to fly with a barnstormer pilot in an open cockpit plane. He loved it, and told his classmates, "A year from now I'll fly myself." Sure enough, he did! Dale got his pilot's license in California in 1937. His instructor, Grant Brown, had been a barnstormer himself and was the husband of our cousin, Angeline Ulberg.

Hitchhiking was a common and cheap way to travel during the thirties. It was safer than in the present era, and the hitchers provided companionship and driving relief on long cross-country trips. Dale did a lot of hitchhiking and met some fascinating people on his journeys to and from California. One older couple liked him so much they wanted to send him to college! One year, he rode back to South Dakota with Donald McKillop, our next-door farm neighbor, who now lived in California. The next year, Dale was picked up in Utah by a college professor, Dr. Ernest Lawrence, from the University of California, Berkeley, who was driving to Minneapolis. Dale didn't know he was driving with the future recipient of the 1939 Nobel Prize for Physics! Our mother was excited when Dale told her of his ride, not because of Dr. Lawrence's academic renown, but because his mother had sung in the Lands Lutheran church choir where she and dad had sung many years ago.

Dale eventually returned to Artesian in 1939. His old boss, John Foote, had bought Quinn's Department Store and had moved his drugstore from across the street into the former men's clothing department. He hired Dale to manage the grocery department. Dale liked working with the clerks, visiting with the customers and learning what he had to do to keep their business. He realized that running a retail business was what he wanted to do with his life.

Dale, Russ, Lorraine

Perhaps what made Dale even happier was the store's new bookkeeper, Beverly Peterson. Bev came from nearby Fedora where she had worked in her father's grocery store. At Foote's, she was in charge of the desk where customers settled their bills with a mixture of cash, credit and the trade of produce, such as eggs. During the Depression, many families had to wait to settle debts until after a good harvest or the selling of livestock. Some bills were never paid. Many families went without rather than go into debt. It was Bev's job to tactfully handle these exchanges of goods and money.

Dale and Bev were both young, good looking and had steady jobs in these troubled times. After a short period of dating, they married on July 14, 1940. Their first home consisted of one large room on the second floor of a private home. The kitchen was in the closet and the rest of the room served for everything else. They ate their noon dinner at the local dentist's home where his wife cooked for others to help supplement her family's income. Later, Dale and Bev moved to the second story of another home. Their rent was minimal. They had no car and walked to wherever they needed to go which wasn't very far in Artesian. If they needed to leave town, they would borrow a car from some relative for that occasion. They lived happily in this apartment and continued working at Foote's Department Store until Dale left to serve in World War II.

Dale and Bev's Wedding
July 14, 1940

Watkins Man

About three times a year, the traveling Watkins man would come to our house to supply our kitchen with vanilla, spices and sundries. Since we saw so few people, his visit was an exciting event! Mother would order a couple of spices, and then he would proceed to show her his new product and, of course, urge her to buy more of his wares. But, with money so tight, she'd not succumb to his glib sales pitch. It seemed he always timed his arrival close to noon so mother would invite him to dinner for which he'd pay her 25 cents. Then the peddler was on his way, both parties happy with their transactions!

Cars and Roads and Roads and Cars

In the 1930s, it was difficult to decide which were in the poorest condition, the roads or the cars. There was no money to improve either one. But farmers needed to have a car to get into town and decent roads to drive on.

Since there were no school buses, our family car was the students' transportation. This meant the car was tied up most of the day, five days a week so all errands into town had to be done after 4:00 p.m. The family tried to consolidate all of this "in town" business in one trip in order to save gasoline, time, and wear and tear on our old Chevy. In those days, one didn't just get in the car and run into town on any little pretext. It was six miles of poor gravel roads and that old car probably didn't go more than 35 mph, spewing gravel all the way.

The weather in spring and winter caused road problems. There were the snowstorms when the road ahead was barely visible. When the snow piled up, the first car out made tracks and the rest followed. If there were a big drift, the driver would floorboard the accelerator hoping to get over that drift without landing in the ditch. Sometimes he just had to wait for the snowplow to come. This could take a day or two, so the family would be snowbound!

When it rained, the single lane country roads without much gravel would get muddy and a car could possibly slip or slide into the ditch! Another hazard was being caught out on the road during a heavy downpour. It was often impossible to see the road so cars stopped until the rain was over. Often the engine wouldn't start because of wet wires. The driver tried to dry them, but if that didn't work, someone would have to walk home to get the tractor and pull that old Chevy home. This seemed to happen only on late Saturday nights when we were so weary we couldn't wait to get home to bed.

During the depression a WPA project was to fix roads. Leo and Vernie were involved in this task. Men could earn $2.50 a day – timekeepers $20.00 a week. If a team of horses was furnished, the pay was $1.00 per day more. There were many mean jokes and cartoons in the newspapers depicting a group of raggedy men by the side of the road leaning on their shovels! Part of the workers' problem was they didn't really have any proper road equipment or sand and gravel to work with. Hence, they were criticized for their seemingly slothful inactivity!

The only paved roads we ever saw were around the cities of Sioux Falls and Mitchell. We often went to Mitchell as it had Montgomery Ward and J.C. Penney where we could shop for clothing and shoes. I remember I'd be so excited when we hit the nice smooth paved road which extended a few miles north of Mitchell. This meant we were almost there after what seemed an eternally long, bumpy journey of twenty-five miles!

Since most families had only one old well-used car, we recognized every-one else's car around Artesian. Everyone had either a Ford or Chevrolet and the least expensive model in the line – no frills. When people saw a Cadillac, Buick or a Packard, their mouths opened, their chins fell down in awe as they stared, speculating on who that rich bugger might be, since he certainly was a stranger in these parts!

The young guys would get in furious debates as to which was the better car, the Chevy or the Ford! They would have little races down the main street to see who could get up the most speed. Not much of a race as these jalopies were pretty old and gutless, but it was their form of fun on a Saturday night! Of course these young men were talking about their family's car that they only occasionally got to drive. It would be a long wait until these teenagers of the 1930s would finally own a car. Most would have to wait until after WWII, after they had come home from service and after the war plants reverted to automobile manufacturing.

Telephones

We had one telephone that hung on the wall. It was an oblong wooden box with a speaker and a listening device that hung on the left side with the ringer handle on the right. We had a party line, which meant that all the patrons who lived in an area shared the same telephone wires. Before we made a call, we would have to listen to check if someone was talking before we rang our party.

Each party had its own distinctive ring. Ours was two long and one short ring, and of course, we knew everyone else's special ring. Many folks, when they heard the telephone ring for a neighbor, spent time listening to their conversation and hearing the latest news. This was called "rubber necking." For a lonely, isolated woman, listening to someone else's business could brighten a dreary day.

If we wanted to call someone in town, we would have to call the operator in Artesian. We'd just have to give a name; she knew all the numbers. If it was a long distance call, the operator would have to call a big city. Then, that operator would call another city until she got to the area we were calling. This could take some time since the lines were often busy.

Russell Eugene Asper
Graduation

Russell Eugene Asper (1920 -   )

By Russell Eugene Asper

I entered this world on October 27, 1920. Our family now consisted of six boys and four girls. Being the youngest, I enjoyed being the center of attention until a week before my seventh birthday. Coming home from school, I received the shock of my young life. I was told to go to the bedroom where I found Mother in bed with a tiny baby. Perhaps my older brothers and sisters had suspected something, but I was young and naive, and this baby came as a complete surprise to me. Obviously this baby was a not a visitor, it was ours, and it was a girl. There was a great deal of discussion of what this baby would be called but when the name "Lorraine" was mentioned, all agreed. Needless to say, there was a great deal of ooing and awing.

I remember my grade school years as very happy, starting out with Jensine Blegraf as my first-year teacher, who roomed and boarded at our home. Another teacher who stands out in my memory is Mrs. Grace Rodee, my fourth-grade teacher. She was very interested in elocution and tried her best to make a public speaker out of me. Each year, there was a Sanborn County Declamation Contest, which was held in Woonsocket. Sadly, I was a big disappointment for her.

Up until 1930, our school had only the children of two families, the Asper's and the Schefsky's, with usually three or four of each family in attendance. That year we gained four new pupils when the Murphy family moved into an old abandoned farmhouse near the school. They were very poor, had really nothing in their house and went barefoot until there was snow on the ground. Their circumstances made an impression on all of us, for although times were getting tough, we all owned farms and had plenty to eat. My sister, Avis, was my teacher in fifth grade. By this time Dale, a seventh grader, and I were the only Asper's left in the school and the three of us would usually walk to school together.

4 Schefsky girls—4 Aspers
?, Russ with dog, Dale, ?
?, Helen, ?, Ernest

73

One of the first things we did in the country school each morning was to fetch a pail of water from a nearby farm to fill our Red Wing crockery water cooler. We also helped with janitorial work, stoking the fire in winter, sweeping floors and so forth. We carried our lunches to school in emptied syrup pails; these lunches usually consisting of a sandwich of homemade bread and meat, a cookie and an apple. When the weather was nice, we played in the yard. Our only play equipment was a seesaw, but we had a bat and ball and often played a game called Ante-Ante Over which consisted of throwing the ball over the shed and hoping the opposite side didn't catch it and tag us.

Russ' New Wagon

At home, I had to do chores after school – gathering eggs, feeding and carrying heavy buckets of water for the chickens. I sometimes milked cows but as I started staying in Artesian at age 14 and working there, I never got into serious farming jobs. Dale and I both left the farm at 14 and except for weekends, never permanently lived at home. When we did come home on weekends, we would crawl into the bathtub and scrub off a week's worth of grime. We could then change into clean clothes that mother had washed and ironed for us and dine on one of her home-cooked meals.

In the fall of 1932, when I was a sixth-grader, our country school was closed due to lack of pupils. Ernest was a senior in high school so he could drive Helen, Dale, and me to school in Artesian. Transportation was always a big problem as cars were few and roads were poor. Town school, with ten or twelve classmates, was a big change for me as I'd often been alone in my grade. I had to adjust to working faster. I realized I had been spending a good share of class time dreaming, waiting for the teacher to get back to me. However, I enjoyed getting to the big town of Artesian and making new friends.

I was fortunate to have had some musical training, taking piano lessons from Bernice Peterson, who I liked very much and who later became my sister-in-law. I practiced just enough to become moderately proficient but this helped me when I started playing the clarinet. I played in the high school band and the summertime town band that entertained the shoppers and visitors on their Saturday evenings in town.

At this time, 1934 and 1935, the country was in the depth of the Great Depression so the government subsidized a housing program for the country students. The boys stayed at the Jones' home while the girls lived at Bill

Thompson's. We had no bathroom—just an outside toilet. We ate our three meals a day in the school lunchroom with food supplied by the government. For the women who worked in the kitchen and the families who provided the rooms, this generated a much-needed income. We would all go home on the weekends. Unfortunately, this government program lasted only one year.

During the summer of my sophomore year, I worked for my brother Vernie at his gas station. We both roomed and boarded at the Brice Hinds home in the west end of town. Mrs. Hinds was a good cook and very neat. Mr. Hinds was something else – a real character. He had a filling station and always kept a small light burning at night, illuminating a sign reading, "If you need gas, knock on the door." I don't remember any takers. In the fall of 1935, I went to work at Quinn's Department Store. Dale had this job but was now going to work at Foote's Drug Store. I was paid three dollars a week for working before and after school and Saturdays from 8 a.m. to 11 p.m. I usually spent Sundays at home. I worked there two years until Dale graduated and left for California to seek his fortune. I then took over Dale's job at Foote's. I now received five dollars a week—a vast improvement. I slept on a cot in the back room where the wallpaper was stored. For the first time, I had a sink and a toilet – and all to myself. My bed covered a trap door to the basement where the liquor supply was stored as Foote had a liquor license. There were robberies taking place in small towns during these desperate times so I served as a cheap night watchman. Fortunately, I was never tested.

I graduated in 1938 without a thought of what I wanted to do except that it wouldn't be farming. Mother was great on all of us getting an education, so she decided I should go to South Dakota State. So, in August, mother, dad, Lorraine and I got into our 1937 Plymouth and started off for Brookings. As I remember it, it was a very hot day but we finally made it to Brookings where we all had lunch at the Rainbow Restaurant, something we'd never done before. We made our way to the Administration Building where I signed up for classes in the fall. There were no job openings at the time but mother was again rooming and boarding a schoolteacher and felt she could contribute this to my educa-

Russ and Lorraine

75

tion. Dad also gave me a little money to start with and Ernest and Margery also helped. Fortunately, tuition was very cheap. There was a cafeteria on the campus where dinner cost 25 cents and my total cost for the year was about $400, including tuition. I lived in a dorm, making many new friends. I still didn't know what I wanted to do, so I took some business courses and got a job at the Agricultural Economics Department for $70 a month. I was now self-sufficient! Perhaps this doesn't sound like much but there were still people unemployed and others supporting families on less than that.

In September 1939, Hitler marched into Poland and the world changed. I took Civil Service exams and applied for a job with the FBI. In early 1940, I received an offer from the FBI with a starting salary of $100 a month! I took the job and moved to Washington, D.C. All male employees started out as messengers before being assigned to a desk job. It was interesting as one would be able to get into the offices of the important people we had read about – agents responsible for capturing notorious criminals of that time – and even the office of the great J. Edgar Hoover. Eventually, I ended up in the Crime Statistics Department where data was collected from the Police and Sheriff's Departments of every city and county in the country. This wasn't as interesting, but it did give me a raise.

I roomed with a friend from Woonsocket, Bob Zieman, who was a cousin of my brother-in-law George Rubida. We lived on the fourth floor of a row house on Rhode Island Avenue. I took a streetcar or walked to work which was less than two miles away. I enjoyed living in Washington and visiting some of the historical sights I had only read about in books. There were a lot of young people in town (about ten girls to every boy) so even I could get a date. Everything was there – movies, orchestras, floorshows, cruising the Potomac, etc.

One leisurely Sunday, while reading the paper, we heard the news of Pearl Harbor and soon the streets were filled with newsboys crying out "Extra, Extra!" Because of my work with the FBI, I had a deferment, but feeling I should do my part, I enlisted in the Navy, but that's another story.

Gold Medal Baby

When I was about 10 months old, Russ suggested to our mother that we should take "our baby" to the State Fair at Huron which occurred in August. The year before, our close neighbor, the Putman's, had taken their baby boy and he had won 1st place! So this evidently inspired Russ to believe that "our baby" could win, too, and I did! I received a 99% minus 1% because of heat rash. Unfortunately, the paper used "Alice" instead of "Lorraine" but thankfully it was engraved correctly on my lovely gold medal.

Alice Asper Is Gold Medal Baby

(Huron Huronite)

Scoring the highest percentage, Alice Eloyce Asper, daughter of Mr. and Mrs. Hans Asper, of Artesian, today was adjudged the most perfect baby in South Dakota.

Alice Eloyce received a gold medal for the distinction of recording as a 99 percent perfect baby. She is 12 months and 8 day sold.

The same baby classed first in the class 1 division and the boy, Darrel Fred Eckman, son of Mr. and Mrs. Fred Eckman, also placed first with a scoring of 98.5 per cent. The babies in this class are between the ages of six months to a year.

There were 123 babies examined, but there were 21, who were not entered in the competitive classes. There were 37 from Huron, 25 from other towns and 61 from the rural sections.

Front of medal

Back of medal

Lorraine Eloyce Asper

Lorraine Eloyce Asper (1927 -   )

I was born at home on the morning of October 20, 1927, with Dr. Loring in attendance. My arrival was a surprise to my ten older brothers and sisters who were seven to 24 years older than I. My siblings had observed that mother was getting a little heavy, but attributed her weight gain to her age. My parents were naturally reticent, and as mother was forty-nine and dad, fifty, they were no doubt embarrassed about this late pregnancy and hadn't informed even their adult children that they were expecting.

Once the shock of my birth was over, the household settled down somewhat. Mother always said that I never had a chance to nap, as everyone wanted to hold and play with the baby. My 12-year-old sister Helen acted as my nanny when she was home from school. The entire family participated in naming me, rejecting Mavis and finally settling on Lorraine Eloyce – wherever that came from!

I believe I was born singing. Mother had been a piano teacher and she and dad both sang in the church choir. On Sunday evenings, when I was older, my mother played the piano and she and dad would sing their favorite hymns which made me feel melancholy. By the time I was eighteen months old, I could sing "She's Got Eyes of Blue" and two other popular songs of the period. I sang "Away in the Manger" as a four-year old young soloist for the Sunday School's Christmas pageant and grade school programs. Four of my siblings – Avis, Margery, Helen and Russell – could play the piano, so there was always someone eager to teach me new songs and rehearse the old.

I learned to entertain myself as my siblings were all too old to play with me and none of our neighbors had children my age. I loved to climb to the top of the chicken coop or hog shed and survey my realm. I would shout, recite poems, and sing my entire repertoire for the chickens, turkeys and pigs even if I didn't get any applause. I played atop the threshing machine pretending it was a store. The long blower served as my counter and imaginary customers stood on the other side. I loved to pet our cat in the barn's hay manger. When she had a new batch of kittens, I'd be excited and want to pet them, but remembered not to touch them as the mother cat might reject her new babies. I helped wean the calves by putting milk in a small bucket, letting the calves suck on my fingers, then lowering their mouths into the milk until they caught on how to drink milk from the pail themselves. I would jump and slide down the high piles of hay in the barn's hayloft, being careful not to fall in a chute and end up on the lower cement floor.

Every summer I would create a playhouse, usually in the basement as this was a cool retreat from the South Dakota summer heat. Sometimes Russell would help carry heavy items or offer his advice on my creation. We'd pile up some boards and create furniture from any odds and ends we could find. Then

I'd gather my dolls together, along with their clothes, bed, table and buggy. Finally, I'd get my own wardrobe together, including old purses and high-heeled shoes, perhaps an old perfume bottle and some rouge and lipstick – all castoffs from my sisters. Then I was ready to play.

I was a very privileged young girl as I had two bedrooms. In the winter, I slept in the bedroom above my parents that had some furnace heat. In the summer, I'd move across the hall to the northeast bedroom which was very cheery and cool. I'd have to move all my belongings there, rearrange the furniture to my liking, make up the bed with a white bedspread and hunt up some rugs. How delightful it was to wake up with the sunshine pouring in my own special room. However, there was one bad aspect about this room. In the summer, we had many severe lightening and thunderstorms. I would become frightened and want to escape to an occupied bed where someone could protect me, but I was too afraid to leave my bed as I thought a great crash of thunder would catch me in the hallway. So, I was betwixt and between!

Because of the Depression, I did not have many toys. My wicker doll buggy and my tricycle were obtained with S&H Green Stamps, a popular retail gimmick to ensure customer loyalty. Most of these stamps were obtained where my sisters bought their clothes. Since I was the baby, I was everyone's favorite. Florence made a bargain with me when I was five, that if I'd stop sucking my thumb, I'd get a big surprise at Christmas. I did conquer my habit and received a rubber dolly with a folding bathinette in which I could put water to bathe her. It was a precious gift for me! When I was eight, Margery gave me a large doll with a cloth body and legs and head made from celluloid. She had blue eyes that would open and close, and she was big enough to wear regular baby clothing. What a special doll... I still have her. I also had a black doll which was unusual in the 1930s. For some unknown reason my dolls never had names. I was a little envious of two of my friends; one had the most popular doll of this era, a Shirley Temple doll, and another had a Lindberg doll carriage copied after the kidnapped Lindberg baby's English pram.

When my older siblings came home for a visit, they'd always have a gift for me, not because I was demanding, but because I was so appreciative and always took good care of my things. When my

Lorraine's S&H Doll Buggy

oldest brother Harvey came home from Woonsocket on weekends, he'd always have a five-cent pack of gum for me. I'd allow myself to have only one stick a day. Often I'd park my gum "on the bedpost overnight," and chew it the next day despite its lack of flavor. I also received Little Big Books and celluloid records for the Victrola with which I could sing along. Occasionally, I'd be happily surprised by my father bringing me a Milky Way candy bar from his trip into town.

I was fortunate to be the beneficiary of three WPA programs. I took piano lessons from Bernice Peterson and elocution lesson from Ruth Thompson (both of whom became my sisters-in-law), all paid for by the government. The third program was a traveling library. There were no public libraries in small rural towns such as Artesian, so this was a real boon. I'd check out five books a week and exchange them for five more the next week. This is how I became an avid reader, as our schools had few outside reading books. I read the Bobbsey Twins, Nancy Drew mysteries, Pearl Buck's on China, etc. My greatest accomplishment was reading the 1,000 page *Gone With the Wind* when I was 12. I was very interested in the relationships between the characters, but had no understanding of the relationship between the North and the South!

My first two years education were spent at the Schaffer School as our home school was closed. My sister Margery was my teacher and she showed me no favoritism! However, before I was old enough for school, she'd often brought the school's printing set and Victrola home which helped me with the alphabet, printing and singing. I don't think I could read when I started school, but readily learned about Dick, Jane and Spot in our first school primer. My only classmate was Eleanor Kneen.

School started at 9:00 a.m., we had an hour for lunch and play, then went home at 4:00 p.m. During recess we'd swing or teeter-totter or play games such as "Mother May I?" and softball. In winter, we'd create snowmen or have a snowball fight. If it was too cold, we'd go down to the basement to eat lunch and perhaps toast marshmallows in the furnace. Every six weeks, each of the pupils memorized a poem and recited it in front of the class – a good lesson in building self-confidence. There were about a dozen pupils in grades 1-8 and Margery controlled them very well. Being in a classroom where one saw the full

SUPERIOR
SANBORN
COUNTY SCHOOLS

AWARDED FOR
Declamation
Lorraine Peper
School Ferguson
Date March 26

scope of elementary study helped the pupils see the entire range of subjects before them and anticipate moving through to the next grade until 8th grade graduation.

When I started third grade, Vernie, Dale, Russell, Margery and I moved into a house in Artesian. Margery had a position at a school south of town. Vernie was working at a gas station. Dale and Russell attended high school and had part time jobs. No one was ever home when I returned to a cold house in the afternoon. The few girls I knew lived on the other side of town and at eight, I was not old enough to walk so far, so I was very lonesome. I was homesick and wanted to stay at home so badly, but my parents refused. I'd go home every weekend and every Sunday afternoon I would start crying. Leo would have to carry me out of the house and put me in the car. I can now understand my parents felt they had no choice, but at the time I certainly felt neglected. I guess the positive aspect of this experience is that I never have suffered from homesickness again.

Happily, the next year the home school reopened and I attended there the next four years. The students consisted of three mean brothers, Pauline Schefsky and myself. Pauline and I loved to read library books sent from the county library and sing duets together. We'd play softball at recess with the boys. Everyone lived close enough to go home for lunch except the teacher

1935 Artesian 3rd and 4th Graders
First (Front) Row: ?, ?, Randall Fisher, ?, ?. Second Row: Daisy Kramer, Glyde Witzel, ?,
Teacher, Dorothy Cassavant, Justine Quinn, Ardis Miller. Third Row: ?, ?,
Elsie Gere, Lorraine Asper, ?. Fourth (Back) Row: ?, Tommy Moe, ?

and me. I knew the teacher, Selma Larsen, well as she lived at our home during the week. After seventh grade, I was sent back to Artesian School for eighth grade, as there would be no other girls at the home school.

In the summer of 1939, our mailman, Charlie Witzel, asked my parents if they would let me go on a ten-day trip to the Black Hills as a companion for their daughter, Glyde. They'd pay for everything but restaurant meals and my spending money. This was a glorious opportunity for me, but coming up with the necessary $12 was a problem. Margery contributed some and the folks managed to scrape together the rest as they felt this was an incredible opportunity for me which it certainly turned out to be. My first big trip!

We spent our first night in Pierre, South Dakota's capital city. We stayed in a very rustic cabin with two double beds and facilities out in back. The first night I couldn't breathe deeply and was awake for a long time – too much excitement, I guess. No doubt the Witzel's thought they had made a bad choice in a traveling companion! The next day we stopped at the now famous Wall Drug, then on to the Bad Lands which looked like a vast wasteland. Next we visited Mount Rushmore which was almost completed. The size of it was awesome and the presidents' faces impressive. I remember swimming in a very hot vast swimming pool at Hot Springs. We traveled on to Rapid City where we visited the Dinosaur Park on a hill, and then drove on to Lead and Deadwood. We also saw a display of rattlesnakes and visited the famous Homestake Gold

1939 Glyde and Lorraine
Dinosaur Park, Rapid City, SD

Mine. We saw the Passion Play, and the Belfouche Rodeo. My first big trip was an incredible experience; one I've always remembered!

When school started that fall, I stayed in Artesian with my brother Vernie and his wife Ruth who lived in the parsonage next to the Lutheran Church about two blocks from school. I no longer felt homesick as I had in third grade. I was very happy as I knew most of the kids at school and liked my first male teacher, Lennart Sundstrom, very much. As an eighth grader, I was selected to sing in the high school choir along with my friend, Elsie Gere. We felt very special as we were the first eighth-graders chosen for this honor.

I spent my freshman year at Vernie's as well. The atmosphere of high school was magic. I loved it! I played clarinet in the band, sang in the glee club and played forward on the basketball team. I wasn't much good but occasionally made a basket. Now that I was living in town, I finally had some girl friends, Glyde Witzel, Elsie Gere and Justine Quinn, and we'd do things together after school and weekends. Glyde and I always went to "the show" on Saturday night no matter what was playing. I'd walk to her house and we'd play games, laugh, talk a lot about clothes and moon over handsome actors. Elsie and I lived only two houses away, so we were in and out of each other's homes often. After school we'd walk downtown to "Annie's Café" and have a nickel hamburger. We thought it was delicious!

Justine was a cousin to my sister-in-law, Ruth. We had good times just being with each other. We'd listen to Glenn Miller's band on the radio every night for fifteen minutes and sing along and dance in Ruth's living room. One night we raised up so much pile from the carpet that Ruth was not happy with us. One afternoon when no one was home, Justine suggested drinking some of Vernie's liquor which we did. She enjoyed it, but not I. Justine and I would enter the declam contest each year with Ruth coaching us. Justine would do drama and I would do humor so we wouldn't compete against one another. We learned to think on our feet and be comfortable in front of an audience.

Looking back, I can see many of the influences which shaped my present life: my love of music, books, travel and my appreciation of a stable, nurturing home.

Electricity

In our sparsely settled area, there was no electricity until the early forties. The Rural Electrification Program didn't come to our parts until much later. We did finally, in the late 30s, get a wind charger which produced enough power for only one or two rooms with one small watt bulb each. Or it could power the radio. Before this, it meant we had no electric lights inside or outside. We lived with kerosene lamps and lanterns.

We had no refrigeration. We had the back porch in the cold season and the cave in the summer to keep our food cool to frozen. The folks couldn't afford a radio for sometime, but eventually the family chipped in to get our parents a small table model. It ran on a battery that only lasted a week or so and then had to be taken to town to be recharged.

A Place at the Table

What a wonderful place our family dining room was! This is where we met three times a day to partake of our daily bread and give thanks for it in prayer. It was a large room with a bay window on the south so it was bright and sunny during the day.

In front of this window Mother had a long two-tiered plant stand where she kept her plants. Her beloved cactus, which I thought was so ugly, sat on it in a large wooden pail. There were geraniums that never bloomed and a few other motley species. I don't think Mother lacked a green thumb; she didn't have the proper soil. The only fertilizers were the barnyard kind and these wouldn't do in the dining room. But she loved her plants and was so proud of them. Sometimes a guest would bring her a new sprout, and she would happily add it to her dreary indoor garden.

Of course, the main focus in this room was the large dining table made of solid oak and, thus, very heavy. It was extended as far as it could go with at least four leaves added in order to accommodate our large family. The table was covered with an oilcloth which was replaced once or twice a year. I always enjoyed the change in patterns and color as they added a little joy to our otherwise drab life. As humble as this cloth might be, it was an object of art in our small world.

Everyone had a specific place at the table. Dad sat at the lower end near the kitchen with the two younger children on either side. I imagine he did this throughout the years. The children changed places when another baby was out of the high chair and old enough to sit at the table. Those "replaced" were bumped up another space. This must have given these children a feeling of importance. They would feel special to become part of the older group, like a rite of passage. There was little talking. Everyone was hungry and concentrated on eating the wholesome and well-prepared dinners and desserts. Most diners had only one helping.

Mother only entertained once or twice a year which was a huge undertaking. She would put a linen cloth on the table. We only had mismatched dishes and silverware; so this everyday tableware had to be used. The linen cloth was the only noticeable difference, but, to the family, it seemed very special.

We had to have two seatings on these Sundays. The five or six guests would be seated with dad and the older children, and we kids would have to wait for the second round. Dishes had to be washed between sittings as there were not enough to go around. We had a crumb tray which was like a little dustpan with brush that would be used to tidy up the cloth before the second seating. I just thought this was an amazing gadget and so special since it was so seldom used.

It was an exciting occasion when we entertained, as we rarely had visitors. I don't believe we served anything extraordinary, probably roast beef, mashed potatoes and gravy which was an ordinary family meal. But perhaps it was special to our town guests. There would be a vegetable and a Jell-O salad plus an array of home-canned beets and cucumber pickles and jams or jellies. One great delight would be Mother's special homemade rolls. No matter what the dessert, it would be smothered in whipped cream. After dinner, the guests visited in the living room and eventually Mother would have time to sit down with them.

No one left empty handed from this Norwegian home. It could be cream, eggs, rolls, cookies, jams or jellies. Even though we had little money, during these hard times, we always had plenty of food and it had to be shared.

It was a long work-filled day with all the preparation and then the cleaning up. Mother would be exhausted but happy to know things had gone so well. Later on, she no doubt would savor all the nice compliments she had received for her lovely dinner served that day. Since eating with the family was customary for us, we never realized the importance of sharing meals together.

Psychologists sometimes question their troubled patients. Where did you sit at the family table? Did you sit down to a well-set table? Did you have a definite place to sit? Did you sit next to someone who was very special to you? Did you pray before you ate? Did some adult lovingly serve you a delicious meal, often with your favorite foods, two or three times a day? Did you feel like you really belonged there? Did you find the sameness of the eating routine assuring or boring? Did you help prepare or clean up after a meal? The answers to these questions reveal much about a person's life.

Experts know that family support patterns and discipline are built into such an everyday common event as "Meal Time." Our two youngest sons used to whine about having to come to the dinner table while their friends could stay out playing. My reply was, "This is how we do it at our home." We've noticed that when we visit our sons in their homes, they all regularly sit down to meals together, so I guess our example was firmly entrenched in their psyche.

When our four sons ranged in age from four to thirteen and were broadening out everyday, Norm and I realized we needed a larger table. What should be our choice but a round oak table just like the one I'd grown up with! I found one at the Junkque Shop in Pharr, Texas. It had three leaves and the price was right, $40.00. I loved that table while our boys were growing up at home and cherish it especially now when they only come for special holidays. We must put in the three leaves again to accommodate ten or more. Norm and I find our happiest moments are when we gather around our old oak table and break bread with our beloved family.

Ole Remmen, Our Norwegian Bachelor

Ole Remmen and his friend Hans Bolstad came from Norway in the early 1900s. They eventually found their way to our area looking for work. Dad hired them and from that time on, they seemed to be part of our family. Later they rented a farm about seven miles north of ours and soon hired a housekeeper, Emma, a recent arrival from Norway. Russell loved going to their house as Emma always had a candy treat saved just for him. Their treat was having a youngster in their home.

We all wondered what would happen with two bachelors and only one woman. Who was going to end up marrying Emma? The "lucky one" turned out to be Hans. The newlyweds soon left the farm, moving near Sioux Falls. As they never had children of their own or close relatives, they were always pleased to see us. When we would stop by on a trip to Sioux Falls, they would invite us to stay to dinner. I'm not sure

Ole Remmen

Hans was the lucky one as I thought Emma's bread was just awful and the rest of her cooking wasn't much better. The grain sacks standing around the main room indicated she wasn't a great housekeeper either.

Ole was now a solo bachelor. He must have felt lonely and isolated in his little house during those long freezing winters. He had few close neighbors and none of his background. He farmed some, but like everyone else in the 1930s, little came of it. He would work by the day for other farmers, especially for my dad. He probably felt at ease with our large Norwegian family and enjoyed speaking his native tongue with my parents and older brothers. The Asper farm was a little haven of comfort for him. Of course, Ole also benefited from mother's good cooking, often staying for both dinner and supper.

Ole had some funny quirks, or at least we kids thought so. Working in the fields during those 1930s summers with temperatures nearing a hundred degrees, Ole would still be wearing his winter long johns. We would speculate on how often he washed his clothes, especially his underwear.

Ole drove to our farm in his early 1920s Model T Ford. He was very proud of that car. When he was working in the fields, I loved to get in and pretend I was driving. The interior was very simple as there was no dashboard, only a steering wheel and the spark lever with a foot-feed, brake and clutch on the floor. To start it, Ole set the spark level, gave it a little gas, then went out in front and cranked the motor until it started. If it didn't start, Ole would methodically start the whole process over again. Another one of his quirks was to slowly walk around the car and kick all four tires before he felt it safe to drive home. We kids would be looking out the bay window, snickering over Ole's exacting procedures.

When our parents moved into Artesian in the early 1940s, Ole moved there also, not too far from our home. Mother did his laundry and usually asked him for Sunday dinner after church. He was always included in our large family functions. Ole never had much to say, but a family gathering wouldn't have been complete without his presence.

Home Cobbling

Shoes were a great and expensive problem during the '30s when buying new ones was often out of the question. Youngsters with growing feet had to have new shoes, or most often, hand-me-downs. The heavy work shoes of most adults had to be repaired at home or not at all.

Dad had a low bench with an iron foot rising up from it. He'd place the worn shoe on the iron foot, then cut a rubber sole to fit on the shoe bottom, which he'd already covered with a sticky glue. These rubber soles were inexpensive, but sometimes leather soles had to be replaced. This was more work, as tiny brads would have to be nailed all around the outside area of the well-worn shoe. These leather soles lasted longer and were only used on the high-top work shoes. Dad became very adept at repairing both men's and women's shoes. Make do or do without!

Privy Information

The outhouse, or privy, was a necessary necessity, but, even so, South Dakota farm folks did not discuss it candidly in my depression-era youth. Nevertheless, the outhouse was regarded as the most important outside building and neither great winds, heavy rain, sleet nor deep snow kept this structure from being used. And in our family of thirteen, it was used often.

I don't recall actual queues outside the outhouse door, but I often saw a sibling glance anxiously out of the west window of our home waiting for the premises to be vacated. He or she would then make a mad dash to the privy, passing the previous occupant contentedly moseying back to the house. We had two well-worn pathways, the back door path leading from the basement then a quick left to the clothesline and this other path beginning at the kitchen door.

Farm families coined many names for this building. It was called "outhouse" as it was one of the farm "out" buildings, fortunately well away from "in the house." Another name was "backhouse," as it was usually set behind the main house where it wouldn't attract attention, but close enough for convenience. The nickname "privy" alluded to the private nature of its function. "The can" was a more vulgar term used mostly by the younger males. "One-, two- or three-holer" indicated the number of seats available.

We had a "three-holer" with one large, one medium and one baby-sized opening. As most of these outhouses had at least two holes, it was not only a place one needed to visit, but also a visiting place. As the youngest child of the family, my mother, a sister or a friend often accompanied me. Intimate conversations took place; hence, two objectives were accomplished at the same time.

Not that the privy's atmosphere was conducive to lingering. The aroma cried for air fresheners, but we had only fresh air. For toilet tissue, we used the daily paper, the *Sears and Roebuck* or *Montgomery Ward* catalogues and old issues of *Colliers* or *Liberty*. *The Saturday Evening Post* was our only source of art as we perused Norman Rockwell's famous covers, at leisure, in this setting. As to the quality of the paper, these non-absorbent, slippery pages left much to be desired.

For sanitary reasons, the outhouse would have to be moved every couple of years. A new pit would be dug just a width away from the old and the outhouse moved to its new position. The fresh dirt from the new pit would be shoveled into the old pit and smoothed off, leaving a deceptively innocent finish. Of course, care had to be taken to position the outhouse correctly in relation to the family well to ensure there would be no seepage into the water supply.

In town on Halloween, the outhouse was one of the favorite targets of male teenaged pranksters. They considered it high humor to knock over a neighbor's outhouse and would compete as to who would administer the final push. Imagine the next morning when the privy's owner rushed out to his comfort station only to find it on its back. He would be furious and eager to cause the culprits as much discomfort as he was feeling. By the end of the morning, neighbor helped neighbor to right all the fallen latrines. But the owners would still be smoldering and discussing whom the pranksters might have been and would plan the next year's vigil – with a shotgun!

Before the advent of the flush toilet, all town buildings had to have privies. Country schools would have two, one for each sex. Since there were no janitors, I remember how we would help the teacher by taking turns sweeping the outhouse, usually on Friday afternoons. All students would be assigned tasks as part of YCL (Young Citizen's League), an organization to help students learn to cooperate in useful tasks. This was a boon to the teacher who not only taught eight grades and stoked the furnace but also was responsible for everything in the school including the upkeep of the outhouse.

When the school near my home reopened after being closed for several years, to my great surprise, we had two new outhouses. They were a WPA project and one of my brothers had helped build them. These privies were "state-of-the-art" for the mid-30s, having a cement foundation, cement stool and wooden seat shaped much like those on a flush toilet. The buildings were of tongue and grove siding painted white. Vents near the top let in fresh air while keeping the flies at bay.

Today it's hard to imagine how excited we all were on opening day to see these new outhouses. My friends and I grew up in the middle of the dust bowl and had seen nothing new built or even painted in our lifetimes. I remember that first day of the new school. I was in fifth grade and had new clothes. It was a big event, seeing those two new buildings painted so sparkling white, perhaps symbolizing a more hopeful future for other things as well.

When indoor plumbing became common for most people, there were still skeptics who kept their outhouses in case something went wrong with that newfangled plumbing. Those who hung on to their relics now own a hot commodity, as old outhouses have sold for thousands of dollars. Little did we anticipate that the privy would become a symbol of nostalgia for America's farming past. I wonder if these outhouse collectors ever really visited one for its intended function, especially on a below-zero South Dakota night.

Artesian – Our Town

When the early settlers started moving into the plains, it was necessary for these people to live fairly close to a village or town. They needed supplies both for farming and for food. Villages usually consisted of a general store which carried little bits of everything the settler might need, and gave him an address so they could send and receive mail. The village of Forestburg had no plan for its streets and people would build a house anywhere. Villages usually had no main road or railroad coming through. There was no city government, but perhaps a small school and a church. However, hamlets provided much needed services for the farmers.

Our town, Artesian, was truly a town as it had a major highway running through it and a depot where the train stopped twice a day. It was the largest town in about a 15-mile radius and had a population of approximately 300 souls. Its streets, though unnamed, were laid out east to west and north to south as straight as a ruler. There was a three-block main street that contained businesses and no houses. It was a typical mid-western small town.

Downtown contained a brick post office where all townspeople received their mail twice daily when the train came in. When some folks heard the train whistle, they'd leisurely stroll down town and stand around chatting with the other residents until the postmaster distributed all of that day's mail. They'd

BIRDS EYE VIEW OF . ARTESIAN. S. DAK. 8   Copyright 1909 Johnson & Bordsen.

take a peek in the glass window of their box, and if there was a letter, they would dial their combination number so the box would open. The two rural carriers would also come to sort the mail for the next day's rural delivery. Albert Peterson delivered the mail to the south, while Charlie Witzel had the northern route – our mailman for many years.

Each block contained a pool hall. The younger crowd would frequent these places to play pool and have a beer. Our father, Hans, didn't approve of these places but he would sit on the benches in front of them and talk with other farmers. As his sons matured into manhood, they frequented the pool hall – especially Ernest who had a penchant for these supposed dens of iniquity. He not only played pool but no doubt had tap beer, too.

The Wise brothers had a furniture/funeral parlor. This gave them something to do between corpses!

Dr. Loring's office was a small building on the main street. Patients could drop in and see him there, but he made house calls as well. He knew the road to our house well between delivering babies and attending family members who had a very serious illness.

Down the side street from them was the telephone company which contained the switchboard and its operator. One could make a call on his own country line, but if he wanted to talk on another line, or someone in Artesian, or a long distance number, he had to go through the operator. Oh how I loved to go there and see that switchboard. It had a lot of holes on the back, while on the desktop, there were wires that had pointed heads that fit into the holes and that's how the operator connected the numbers. As a little girl I felt this would be a wonderful job. I visited so often when I came into town, I was almost a pest.

In the thirties, there was only one car dealer left in Artesian. Mr. Jones sold Chrysler products, i.e. Plymouth, Dodge, DeSoto and Chryslers from his garage on south main street which was the end of the other business district. Needless to say, the low-end Plymouth would be the best seller. Most people couldn't afford new cars. They bought a second-hand Ford or a Chevy which were even less expensive. In those days to see an expensive car such as a Cadillac stop in our town left all the citizens agog!

The Johnson Hotel occupied the center of town. During the mid-thirties, it had little business. Since the economy was so bad in the 30s, traveling salesmen no longer came to stay at the hotel. However, the hotel sold treats. A dish of ice cream would be served in a round silver dish with a round ice cream spoon and a sugar wafer stuck jauntily on the top. I was enthralled by this kind of grandeur. I only had this treat three or four times as ten cents was too much to spend when you could buy a cone for a nickel, or Mrs. Johnson could fill a bag up with candy that would last much longer.

There were usually a couple of restaurants in town, but our family never ate a meal out, as we couldn't afford it. Dale and Russ worked in Artesian, ate out only two meals a day, spending no more than a total of two or three dollars a week on food.

Sometime before the Great Depression started, a nice brick movie theater was built, but it was never opened. About 1934, right in the midst of the worst hardships, it was opened! Movies cost $0.25 adults and $0.10 children – almost affordable.

There were many pictures being made in Hollywood which were often of the very rich and elegant who lived in fancy apartments and wore beautiful clothes that no South Dakotan had every seen! The movie industry knew that this make-believe dream world was what the public needed and wanted as it lifted depressed spirits for an hour or two in these hard pressed times. Ginger Rogers wearing a flowing white satin dress and Fred Astaire in top hat and tails seemingly danced on air across the screen. Cary Grant and Adolph Menjou struck poses of very sophisticated, well dressed, wealthy gentlemen. But there was also the mangy Margery Main and the bumbling Wallace Berry who made us laugh. Of course, cowboy movies with Gene Autry and Hopalong Cassidy were favorites too.

The theater was really a boon to Artesian, as people from other nearby towns would come to shop as well as to see the movie. The same movie was shown twice on Saturday and Sunday nights. I often went both nights and did not have to pay the second night. I was a movie fan of the first order.

Later, when the theater realized how much the public liked the movies, they held one on Wednesday night and had a drawing for dishes or cash. My mother loved this and even won a few dollars once! She loved the movies, too, but dad never attended them but was not upset with our attendance. The movies were such a wonderful experience for these needy people at this severe period of time for few had ever traveled beyond their homestead and town. It provided a means of communication and education they had never encountered before. It gave them a ray of hope, something outside themselves to think about during the week.

Across the street from the theater was the building that housed our weekly paper, *The Artesian Commonwealth*. The town's people waited anxiously for Thursday, as that was the day the press ran. The front page, unlike the daily paper, did not attempt to tell worldwide stories, but kept to the subject of the area that would be interesting to the locals. Inside pages would have obituaries, weddings, church announcements, grocery store ads and sometimes a picture or two. Social items would be included too, even though everyone knew who, what, where and why it took place but it pleasured them to see it in print. There were other news items from nearby towns for those subscribers.

Next door to the newspaper office stood the bandstand. On summer Saturday nights, the high school band played; the people would stand around listening unless they were fortunate enough to have parked their cars close enough so they could sit at ease and enjoy the concert. Russ played clarinet and Dale, the trombone, so they'd have permission to get off from work for an hour on this busy night in order to play with the band. It provided a nice bit of culture for a small town.

The drug store had a pharmacist, John Foote, who provided prescription drugs since there were few over-the-counter kind. Best of all in the back of the store was a huge elegant mirror held up by marble pillars. It was always cool and dark there and the ambiance made one feel very special.

Artesian had five churches – Lutheran, Catholic, Methodist, Presbyterian and Wesleyan Methodist which we called the Holy Rollers.

Three gas stations serviced all the cars in the area – two on the highway and one two blocks south that Vernie owned. The gas pump had a round glass top that had to be pumped full. When gasoline was being put in the car tank, you could look at the glass to read the marks showing how many gallons it took. Stations sold oil, gasoline and tires while a few had repair shops which made it a very simple operation. Some stations had a cold drink chest that was filled with ice, Orange, root beer and Coca Cola were the favorite cold pops. Most people didn't use ice, so in the midst of scorching summer days, cold pop was a special treat!

There were two grocery stores. One was fairly small and sold only groceries and meats. The larger one was a combination of grocer, dry goods – both men and women's clothing. The only cold show case was the meat counter while everything else bought was dried or canned, with some fresh "wilted" vegetables and bread was delivered twice a week.

A one-man barbershop – "shave and a hair cut – two bits". Not only did the hair get pretty deep by the end of the day, but a lot of the stories too!!!!

The lumberyard was one block west of the main street and ran along next to the highway. It supplied the customers with their lumber, nails and fencing needs. A hardware store was also part of the town. It was eventually closed when a chain store, Gambles, came in, as its merchandise was less expensive.

Along the highway were two grain elevators. This is where the farmers brought their grain to be tested for its quality. Here, they faced the truth about the paltry amounts of bushels their land had produced and the puny check they received for all their hard work.

A nice brick corner building housed the bank. During the Depression, it couldn't have done much business excepting for the farmers attempting to negotiate loans to save their farms. That option could only have been in the very early thirties for as time went on, farming conditions only grew worse with no improvement in the foreseeable future.

The city had a building that housed the fire equipment used by the volunteer firemen. This building also had a one-room jail cell. It was probably never used, as the crime statistics were nil. The city fathers met there to discuss the town's welfare with the Mayor presiding. Vernie served as Mayor at one time.

Artesian had a park with trees and picnic tables. There was a large swimming pool that the town kids used and enjoyed all summer long. Country kids seldom got to use the pool as this was busiest time on the farm, so no one had time to drive them to town.

About a mile north of Artesian was the town cemetery, Mount Pleasant. It had a fence around it, an attractive gate and was well kept. Memorial Day was a big occasion. The graves were decorated; there would be a program, with prayers, a reciting of "In Flanders Field", a singing of "The Star Spangled Banner" and a patriotic speech. Despite the fact, it was usually a very hot day, many people attended attired in their best clothes. In the 30s, I was fascinated by the pomp and circumstance of this occasion, but unlike most of my friends, I had no one buried there. Now if one visits Mount Pleasant, they will find many Asper markers.

Hot Water Sponge Cake

Hot Water Spong Cake.
4 eggs(beaten lightly)- 1½ cup sugar.
beat again) 2 cups flour a pinch of salt
2 teaspoons baking powder- 1 tps vanilla
beat good. 1 cup boiling water added
last; bake in a loaf pan. Sprinkel
sugar over cake back 35 to 40 minutes.

Written in mother's own hand

Grandma Asper's Cookie Recipes

SUGAR COOKIES

Cream:
3-1/2 sticks oleo or butter
2 cups sugar
Beat:
2 eggs

Add:
5 cups sifted flour
1 t soda
1 t cream of tartar
1/2 t salt
2 t vanilla

Mix all together
Make round balls the size of a walnut
Place on baking sheet, press lightly
Then mark with a fork
Bake at 375° for 10 min.
Makes 4-1/2 doz.

BROWN SUGAR COOKIES

Cream:
2 cups brown sugar
1 cup oleo or butter

Add:
2 beaten eggs
2 t soda
2 t cream of tartar
2 t vanilla
3-1/2 cups sifted flour

Mix well
Roll balls the size of a walnut
Then mark with a fork
Bake at 375° for 10 min.

REFRIGERATOR COOKIES

Cream:
1/2 brown sugar
1/2 white sugar
1/2 cup butter or oleo
1 egg beaten
1 t vanilla
1/2 t soda
1/2 t cream of tartar
1-3/4 cup sifted flour

Mix well and add:
1/2 cup chopped nuts

Form dough into long oval shape
Refrigerate for 2 hours
Slice thin and bake at 375° for 10 min.
Save some dough to bake later

CHOCOLATE DROP COOKIE (Avis)

Sift together:
2 cups cake flour
1-1/2 baking powder
1/4 t soda
1/4 t salt

Cream:
1/2 cup butter or oleo
2/3 cup brown sugar
1 egg, beaten
1-1/2 sq. unsweetened baking
   chocolate, melted
1/2 cup milk
1 t vanilla

Mix all ingredients lightly
Add:
1/2 cup chopped nuts

Bake 375° for 8 min.
Frost with powder sugar icing

98

Norwegian Christmas Foods

SPRITS

Cream thoroughly:
1-1/2 cup butter (3/4#)
1 cup sugar

Sift together:
1 t baking powder
3-3/4 cups sifted flour

Add:
1 well-beaten egg
2 t vanilla

Add all to batter. Force through cookie press. Bake a cookie or two to test consistency of batter. If the shapes don't hold, add a small amount of flour until they do.

Bake at 375° to 400° for 8 to 10 minutes. Cookies should not be brown so watch carefully. Makes 4 dozen.

FATTIGMAND

1 cup sugar
1/2 cup butter
2 eggs

6 T sweet cream
1 t vanilla

Combine ingredients, cool, roll dough on floured board to less than 1/4" thick Cut in strips 1-1/2" by 4". Cut slit in middle drawing one end through slit. Fry in hot oil until very lightly browned. Use a slight powered sugar coating if desired. Keep enclosed in container. Fattigmand gets better with age.

BERLINERKRANSER

Cream:
1 cup butter
2 hard-boiled yolks

Add:
1/2 cup sugar
2 raw egg yolks

Sift in 2 cups flour and work into long small rolls. Form dough into pencil size rings.

Dip rings into partially beaten egg white and sprinkle with chopped blanched almonds or coarse white sugar.

Bake at 350° until a delicate brown.

LUTEFISK

Buy your lutefisk at a specialty fish market. Let them advise you how much lutefisk you need. Take home and soak the lutefisk in mild salted water over night. Rinse and soak in clear cold water for five hours. Drain well. Put fish into cheesecloth bags, filling bags half full. Drop bags into boiling, salted water boiling for 5 min. Remove bags from water and drain. Skin and bone fish with a spoon. Keep fish warm and serve with melted butter.

LEFSE

4 lbs. potatoes, peel boil until done, drain
Add:
2 T shortening
1 T salt
Mash potatoes, then cool thoroughly
Add:
1 cup flour to make dough that can be rolled out easily (as thin as piecrust)

Shape mixture into 24 balls (cooler the better)
Roll each ball very thin using as little flour as possible (too much flour or too low heat makes lefse tough).
Bake on an electric grill on moderately high heat, turn to other side.
Makes 24, 8" lefse.

KJOTKAKER (NORWEGIAN MEAT BALLS)

2-1/2 lbs. round steak
1/2 onion, sauted in
butter
1/2 lb. Pork
1 t baking powder

2-1/2 t salt, 1/4 t pepper
1 cup cream
1/8 t nutmeg
1 beaten egg

Grind meats very fine, add all other ingredients to meat mixture beating thoroughly until very light in texture. Form into small, light balls, brown in butter. Make gravy from the drippings, then replace meatballs and cook or bake slowly 1/2 hour or so.

Asper Family Health Chart

Family diseases are important for future generation to know. During the last thirty or so years, genetic scientists have discovered how our genes are in essence a picture of our ancestors. It is well for us to know about our inherited diseases in order to apprise our doctors when they ask us to record our family history.

LIST OF THE ASPER FAMILY DISEASES:

Alcoholism

Alzheimer's Disease

Cancer

Carotid Arteries

Dyslexia

Glaucoma

Heart Disease: Heart Attack – Heart Failure – Angina

High Blood Pressure

Migraine Headaches

Narcolepsy

Scoliosis

Osteoporosis – A thinning of the bones is a highly susceptible to those of Norwegian ancestry. The thinning of bones results in hip and knee surgery.

The Asper-Hanson union produced very good genes. They live long lives with good health. Of the diseases mentioned above, most have scant numbers. The three most common diseases are alcoholism, high blood pressure and dyslexia.

MAP OF NORWAY

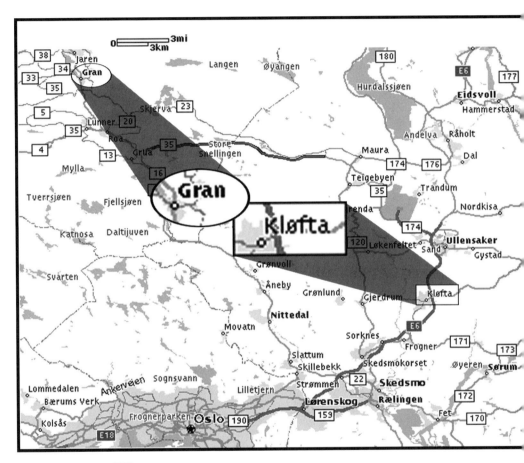

⬭ Gran – Milda's mother's birthplace in Norway

▭ Klofta – Asper family homestead

ASPER—GENEOLOGY

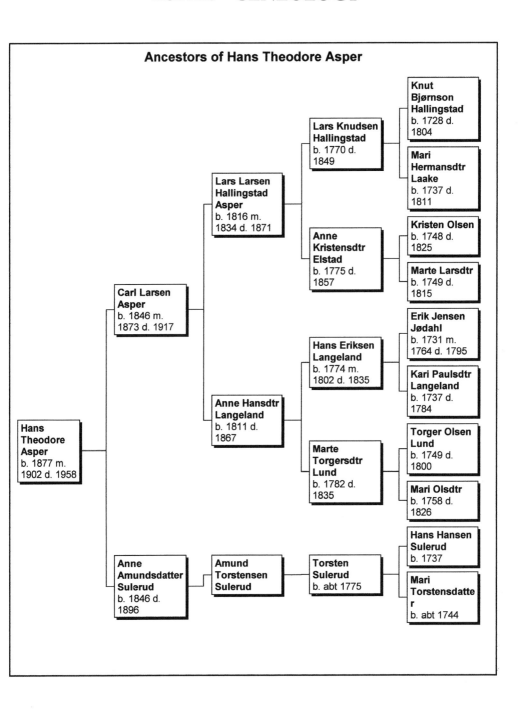

Ancestors of Hans Theodore Asper

Hans Theodore Asper b. 1877 m. 1902 d. 1958

- **Carl Larsen Asper** b. 1846 m. 1873 d. 1917
  - **Lars Larsen Hallingstad Asper** b. 1816 m. 1834 d. 1871
    - **Lars Knudsen Hallingstad** b. 1770 d. 1849
      - **Knut Bjørnson Hallingstad** b. 1728 d. 1804
      - **Mari Hermansdtr Laake** b. 1737 d. 1811
    - **Anne Kristensdtr Elstad** b. 1775 d. 1857
      - **Kristen Olsen** b. 1748 d. 1825
      - **Marte Larsdtr** b. 1749 d. 1815
  - **Anne Hansdtr Langeland** b. 1811 d. 1867
    - **Hans Eriksen Langeland** b. 1774 m. 1802 d. 1835
      - **Erik Jensen Jødahl** b. 1731 m. 1764 d. 1795
      - **Kari Paulsdtr Langeland** b. 1737 d. 1784
    - **Marte Torgersdtr Lund** b. 1782 d. 1835
      - **Torger Olsen Lund** b. 1749 d. 1800
      - **Mari Olsdtr** b. 1758 d. 1826
- **Anne Amundsdatter Sulerud** b. 1846 d. 1896
  - **Amund Torstensen Sulerud**
    - **Torsten Sulerud** b. abt 1775
      - **Hans Hansen Sulerud** b. 1737
      - **Mari Torstensdatter** b. abt 1744

Hans Theodore Asper b. 4 Jul 1877 Canton, Lincoln Co., SD
d. 13 Apr 1958 Artesian, Lincoln Co., SD
+ **Milda Berthina Hanson** b. 2 Sep 1878 , Lincoln Co., SD
  m. 26 Nov 1902
  d. 23 Aug 1973 Artesian, , SD
    ① **Avis Marscella Asper** b. 29 Oct 1903 Alcester, Union Co., SD
      d. 9 May 1996 Morgan Hill, , CA
      + **George Rubida** b. 18 Jan 1901
        m. 18 Jan 1935
        d. 5 Oct 1950
        ① **Darrell Authier Rubida** b. 10 Feb 1937 Mitchell, , SD
          + **Loretta Christine Sweet** b. 2 May 1936 Oklahoma City, , OK
            m. 8 Jun 1963 Reno, , NV
            ① **Pamela Avis Rubida** b. 4 Jan 1964 Los Gatos, , CA
              + **Myron John Von Raesfeld** b. 20 Jan 1961 San Jose, , CA
                m. 20 Jun 1987 Santa Clara, , CA
                ① **Jason Scott Von Raesfeld** b. 11 Aug 1988 Santa Clara, , CA
                ② **Alexandra Von Raesfeld** b. 30 Mar 1990 Santa Clara, , CA
                ③ **Michelle Von Raesfeld** b. 22 Jul 1991 Santa Clara, , CA
                ④ **Jamie Von Raesfeld** b. 16 Jun 1993 Santa Clara, , CA
                ⑤ **Courtney Claire Von Raesfeld** b. 25 Sep 1996 Santa Clara, , CA
                ⑥ **Zachary John Von Raesfeld** b. 23 Nov 1999
            ② **Christine Deanne Rubida** b. 14 Apr 1969 Santa Clara, , CA
              + **Christopher Lane** b. 14 Nov 1962
                m. 6 Aug 1989 Los Gatos, , CA
                ① **Breanna Ashley Lane** b. 23 Jun 1990 Santa Clara, , CA
                ② **Melanie Nicole Lane** b. 17 Mar 1992 Santa Clara, , CA
        ② **Dennis Asper Rubida** b. 8 Aug 1940 Mitchell, , SD
          + **Diane Marilyn Olstad** b. 13 May 1943 , , MN
            ① **Denise Rubida** b. 16 Aug 1966 Los Gatos, , CA
              + **Garth Brown** m. 16 Jul 1993 Lake Tahoe, , CA
                ① **Tess Diane Brown** b. 29 Jul 2000
            ② **Danielle Alyse Rubida** b. 27 May 1968 Santa Clara, , CA
              + **Mickey Taylor** m. 8 Oct 2004
      + **Harvey Threadgold** m. 18 Jun 1959
    ② **Harvey Clayton Asper** b. 27 Apr 1905 Artesian, , SD
      d. 17 Jul 1957
      + **Helen Ruml** b. 25 Nov 1912
        m. 8 Nov 1945
        d. 25 Nov 1976
        ① **Janice Marie Asper** b. 4 Jul 1947
          d. 21 Sep 1998
        ② **Judy Louise Asper** b. 29 Oct 1949 Mitchell, , SD
          + **Roger Merle Rae** b. 1 Jun 1950 Rock Rapids, , IA
            m. 23 Jul 1972
            ① **Nicolas Edward Rae** b. 3 Mar 1977 Sioux Falls, , SD
              + **Marie Krell** b. 1 Sep 1978
                m. 26 Jun 2003
            ② **Alexis Louise Rae** b. 20 Nov 1980 Sioux Falls, , SD
        ③ **Jean Milda Asper** b. 24 Mar 1952 Mitchell, , SD
          + **James R. Stordahl** m. 1971

1   **2**   **3**   **4**   **5**

Hans Theodore Asper
② **Harvey Clayton Asper**

Div.
　　　① **Lisa Marie Stordahl** b. 12 Jan 1972 Rapid City, , SD
　　　② **Lesley Jean Stordahl** b. 29 Aug 1976 Coco Solo, , Panama Canal Zon, PANA
　　+ **Kenneth E. Anderson** b. 22 Sep 1950 Alameda, , CA
　　　m. 3 Jul 1990 Woonsocket, , SD
　　　① **Sydney Carole Anderson** b. 17 Mar 1991 Auburn, , NE
③ **Leo Paul Asper** b. 22 Oct 1906 Artesian, , SD
　d. 13 Jul 1969 Artesian, , SD
　+ **Bernice Peterson** b. 22 Aug 1905
　　m. 1 Jun 1940 Woonsocket, , SD
　　d. 19 May 1988
　　① **Albert Leo Asper** b. 4 Mar 1941 Mitchell, , SD
　　　+ **Vergie Voelzke** b. 24 Oct 1945
　　　　m. 23 Dec 1966
　　　　① **ElizaBeth Marie Asper** b. Jun 1975
　　　　② **Paul David Asper** b. 14 Nov 1978
　　② **David Paul Asper** b. 27 Jun 1945 Mitchell, , SD
　　　+ **B. Kaye Herbert** b. 6 Feb 1947
　　　　m. 30 May 1969
　　　　① **Katherine Betia Asper** b. 6 Feb 1976
　　　　② **Jayne Valere Asper** b. 19 Sep 1979
④ **Vernie Burdette Asper** b. 10 Aug 1908 , Lincoln Co., SD
　d. 29 Sep 1992 Canton, Lincoln Co., SD
　+ **Ruth Elaine Thompson** b. 30 Jul 1912 Artesian, Sanborn, SD
　　m. 25 Dec 1936 Artesian, , SD
　　d. 21 May 1991 Brookings, Brookings, SD
　　① **Audrey Elaine Asper** b. 1 Sep 1939 Mitchell, Davidson Co., SD
　　　+ **Harlyn Lee Threadgold** b. 4 Sep 1936 Mitchell, Davidson Co., SD
　　　　m. 14 Aug 1956 Artesian, , SD
　　　　① **Lee Kent Threadgold** b. 30 Mar 1957 Mitchell, Davidson Co., SD
　　　　　+ **Cynthia Sue Thielson** b. 23 Jul 1957 Arcadia, , CA
　　　　　　m. 17 Jun 1978 Brookings, , SD
　　　　　　① **Adam Lee Threadgold** b. 5 Jul 1979 Madison, Lake Co., SD
　　　　　　② **Karli Marie Threadgold** b. 27 Jul 1981 Madison, , SD
　　　　　　③ **Carrie Ann Threadgold** b. 10 Aug 1983 Madison, , SD
　　　　　　④ **Eric Michael Threadgold** b. 6 Feb 1989 Madison, , SD
　　　　② **Laurie Ruth Threadgold** b. 19 Sep 1959 Brookings, Brookings Co., SD
　　　　　+ **Keith Huelsebusch** b. 7 Apr 1952 St. Louis, , MO
　　　　　　m. 2 May 1987 St. Louis, , MO
　　　　　　① **Tyler James Huelsebusch** b. 31 Jan 1990 St. Louis, , MO
　　　　　　② **Tara Lynn Huelsebusch** b. 2 Aug 1992 St. Louis, , MO
　　　　③ **Lynn Michele Threadgold** b. 30 Oct 1970 Yankton, Yankton Co., SD
　　　　④ **Lou Ann Threadgold** b. 5 May 1974 Yankton, Yankton Co., SD
　　　　　+ **Chad Janzen** b. 1974
　　　　　　m. Aug 1997
　　② **Janet Lorraine Asper** b. 3 Feb 1945 Mitchell, , SD
　　　+ **Russell E. Gurley** b. 14 Jan 1945 Oroville, , CA
　　　　m. 6 Jul 1968 Brookings, , SD
　　　　Div.

1　　2　　3　　4　　5

Hans Theodore Asper
④ **Vernie Burdette Asper**
② **Janet Lorraine Asper**

    ① **Derinda D. Gurley** b. 1 Jan 1970 Sacramento, , CA
  ③ **Neal Evan Asper** b. 26 Jan 1949 Mitchell, , SD
  + **Mary Hegstrom** b. 16 Oct 1951 Watertown, , SD
    m. 26 Jun 1971 Brookings, , SD
    Div.
    ① **Jennifer Asper** b. 4 Dec 1971 Brookings, , SD
    + **Greg Springer** b. 29 Jul 1968 OR
      m. 1 Aug 1998 Portland, OR
      ① **Cameron Springer** b. 13 Dec 2000 Portland, OR
      ② **Trey Springer** b. 31 May 2003
  + **Sherry Mae Ann Walters** b. 22 Jul 1957 Lake Preston, , SD
⑤ **Florence Louise Asper** b. 4 Sep 1910 Artesian, , SD
+ **Donald Vernon Lukehart** b. 17 Nov 1910
m. 3 May 1933
d. 1 Jul 1997 Hemet, , CA
  ① **Donald Leo Lukehart** b. 5 Nov 1933 Sioux Falls, , SD
  d. 1 Jul 1997 Hemet, , CA
  + **Barbara Jeanette Byrd** b. 2 Nov 1933
    ① **Gregg Lawrence Lukehart** b. 27 Sep 1952 San Jose, , CA
    d. 24 May 1991 San Diego, , CA
    + **June Mary Gutowski** b. 5 Jun 1953 Paterson, , NJ
      m. 24 Jun 1971 San Diego, , CA
      ① **Tina Marie Purdy** b. 27 Feb 1973 Okinawa, , , Japan
      + **Michael Lee Marshall** b. 24 Apr 1972 San Diego, , CA
        ① **Darren Lee Marshall** b. 6 Nov 1994 Sacramento, , CA
      + (---) (---)
        ① **Sidney Taylor Leman** b. 24 Dec 2003
      ② **Melissa Dawn Purdy** b. 5 Nov 1975 Sacramento, , CA
  + **Glenda Sharon De Bolt** b. 10 Jun 1935 Arbuckle, , CA
  m. 2 Dec 1955 San Jose, , CA
    ① **Timothy Donald Lukehart** b. 2 Dec 1956 Chico, , CA
    + **Sarah Jane Hoskins** b. 16 Apr 1958 Piedmont, , CA
      m. 23 Jul 1983 Sacramento, , CA
      ① **Amanda Jane Lukehart** b. 3 Aug 1984 Sacramento, , CA
      ② **Paige Jane Lukehart** b. 16 Jun 1986 Sacramento, , CA
      ③ **Bocefus Timothy Lukehart** b. 17 Oct 1988 Sacramento, , CA
    ② **Jody Richard Lukehart** b. 4 Sep 1959 Bakersfield, , CA
    + **Deborah Lynn Dunn** b. 20 May 1962 Paconia, , CA
      m. 30 Aug 1986 Sacramento, , CA
      ① **Spencer Otto Lukehart** b. 19 Sep 1990 Sacramento, , CA
      ② **Tucker Nicholas Lukehart** b. 31 Jan 1993 Sacramento, , CA
    ③ **Hugh Allen Lukehart** b. 25 Dec 1962 Sacramento, , CA
    + **Tracy Lynn Karnes** b. 15 Nov 1964 Long Beach, , CA
      m. 22 Aug 1987 Sacramento, , CA
      ① **Jessalee Lukehart** b. 31 Jan 1988 Sacramento, , CA
      ② **Amos Wolfgang Lukehart** b. 5 May 1989 Sacramento, , CA
      ③ **Raven Marie Lukehart** b. 14 Oct 1991 Vacaville, , CA
    ④ **Sherie Diane Lukehart** b. 16 Sep 1964 Sacramento, , CA

1   2   3   4   5   6

    + Robin Edward Graysmark b. 13 Nov 1959 Toronto, , ON, CAN
     m. 17 Jun 1989 Woodland, , CA
      ① **Ryan Spencer Graysmark** b. 25 Sep 1993 Santa Clara, , CA
      ② **Emma May Graysmark** b. 1 May 1996
  ② **Gloria Adele Lukehart** b. 16 Nov 1934 Worthington, , MN
  + John Gates Saffery b. 10 Jun 1933 Hartford, , CT
   m. 3 Aug 1957 West Palm Beach, , FL
   d. 17 Mar 1976 San Jose, , CA
    ① **Diana Jean Saffery** b. 4 May 1960 Sayama-Shi, , , Japan
    + Robert John Wagner b. Jul 1953 , , NJ
     m. 6 Oct 1986 Monterey, , CA
      ① **Ryan Justin Wagner** b. 8 Jan 1984 San Jose, , CA
      ② **Jayson Tyler Wagner** b. 23 Oct 1985 San Jose, , CA
    ② **Darrick Lance Saffery** b. 23 Sep 1961 Sayama-Shi, , , Japan
     d. 7 Apr 1994 Seattle, , WA
  ③ **Gerald Dennis Lukehart** b. 21 Jan 1936 Sioux Falls, , SD
  + Mary Madeline Degalke b. 12 Feb 1937
   m. 7 Jul 1956 San Jose, , CA
    ① **Daniel D. Lukehart** b. 24 Feb 1958 Corvallis, , OR
    + Teri Ann Meece b. 17 Sep 1961 Boise, , ID
     m. 17 Sep 1983
      ① **Taylor Lukehart** b. 18 Oct 1988 Fairfield, , CA
      ② **Dustin Lukehart** b. 23 Sep 1991 Fairfield, , CA
      ③ **Dillon Lukehart** b. 24 Apr 1993 Fairfield, , CA
    ② **Rozelind A. Lukehart** b. 24 Feb 1958 Corvallis, , OR
    + Joseph Holman b. 25 Jul 1958
     m. 7 Aug 1977 Naches, , WA
      ① **Lacey Holman** b. 30 Jul 1984 Yakima, , WA
      ② **Austin Holman** b. 22 Apr 1987 Yakima, , WA
      ③ **Mary Clara Holman** b. 27 Apr 1995 Yakima, , WA
    ③ **Dainard R. Lukehart** b. 11 Feb 1962 San Jose, , CA
    + Linda Vanderlinden m. 11 Aug 1989 Yakima, , WA
      ① **Nicholas Lukehart** b. 26 Sep 1990 Yakima, , WA
      ② **Blake Allen Lukehart** b. 9 Sep 1996
  ④ **Roger Allen Lukehart** b. 25 May 1938
  + Eva Anna-Greta Sjoberg b. 18 Jul 1931 Stockholm, , , Sweden
   m. 17 Aug 1963
    ① **Moriet Lisa Lukehart** b. 11 Sep 1966
    + Edward Miketa m. 16 Sep 1989
      ① **Marley Autumn Miketa** b. 9 Nov 1996 Bellevue, , WA
      ② **Lauren Elsie Miketa** b. 14 May 2000
    ② **Erik Matts Lukehart** b. 22 Nov 1967
  ⑤ **Vivienne Joy Lukehart** b. 20 Apr 1940 Rochester, , MN
  + William Arthur Anderson b. 20 Mar 1937 Pierre, , SD
   m. 20 Aug 1958 Virginia City, , NV
    ① **ElizaBeth Marie Anderson** b. 21 Sep 1959 San Jose, , CA
    + Kent Edwin Parker b. 20 Aug 1957 Grand Junction, , CO
     m. 12 Mar 1979

◄ **2** **3** **4** **5**

Hans Theodore Asper
⑤ **Florence Louise Asper**
⑤ **Vivienne Joy Lukehart**
① **ElizaBeth Marie Anderson**

⑴ **Chad Jacob Parker** b. 18 Aug 1981 San Jose, , CA
d. 2 Apr 2000
⑵ **Lindsey Renee Parker** b. 18 Nov 1984 San Jose, , CA
⑵ **Guy William Anderson** b. 18 Nov 1960 San Jose, , CA
+ **Mary Peterson** b. 21 Aug 1962 St. Paul, , MN
m. 12 May 1984 Saratoga, , CA
⑴ **(---) Danielle Marie** b. 29 Apr1998
⑵ **Matthew William Anderson** b. 20 Feb 2000
⑶ **Rachelle Louise Anderson** b. 14 Jan 1962 San Jose, , CA
+ **Jimmy Sindle** b. 26 Mar 1945 Fordice, , AR
m. 29 Jul 1984 Tahoe, , CA
⑴ **Nicholas Travis Sindle** b. 24 Dec 1984
⑵ **Mitchell William Sindle** b. 24 Dec 1987
⑥ **Margery Hortense Asper** b. 16 Jul 1912 Artesian, , SD
d. 3 Feb 1994
+ **Lloyd Cook** b. 1 Apr 1910
m. 16 Jun 1938
d. 1 Apr 1958
+ **Roy Maack** m. 14 Feb 1960
⑦ **Ernest Wilbert Asper** b. 28 Jan 1914 Artesian, , SD
d. 28 Apr 1960
+ **Patricia June Burchfield** b. 7 Aug 1925
m. 8 Dec 1952
⑴ **Lennis Larry Asper** b. 8 Feb 1953
⑧ **Helen Pauline Asper** b. 12 Nov 1915 Artesian, Sanborn Co., SD
+ **Robert Demers Cullerton (Sr.)** b. 30 Jun 1918 Butte, , MT
m. 1 Feb 1944 d. 21 Apr 1998
⑴ **Robert Demers Cullerton (Jr.)** b. 4 Mar 1945 Butte, , MT
+ **Mary ElizaBeth Davidson** b. 20 Dec 1945 Des Moines, , IA
m. 26 Aug 1967 Prairie Village, , KS
⑴ **John Demers Cullerton** b. 27 Nov 1970 Portsmouth, , VA
+ **Julia Lynn Prather** m. 19 Apr 1997
⑴ **Clara Anita Cullerton** b. 21 May 2001 Newark, DE
⑵ **Robert John Cullerton** b. 2 Jul 2003 Atlanta, GA
⑵ **Anne Dawson Cullerton** b. 28 Nov 1975 St. Louis, , MO
⑵ **Sally Ann Cullerton** b. 13 Jun 1946 Butte, , MT
+ **James Davis** m. May 1965
Div.
⑶ **Pamela Marie Cullerton** b. 6 Oct 1947 Helena, , MT
+ **Dennis D. Prater** b. 8 Jun 1947 Olathe, , KS
m. 9 Jun 1969 Prairie Village, , KS
⑴ **Derek D. Prater** b. 8 Aug 1973 St. Johnsbury, , VT
⑵ **Scott B. Prater** b. 25 Sep 1975 Lawrence, , KS
+ **Gary D. Nuzum** b. 7 Apr 1950 Fall City, , NE
m. 15 Jun 1986 Lawrence, , KS
⑨ **Dale Raymond Asper** b. 14 Oct 1917 Artesian, , SD d. 26 May 2004
+ **Beverly Peterson** b. 26 Jul 1920 Fedora, , SD

1   2   3   4   5

Hans Theodore Asper

      m. 14 Jul 1940 Woonsocket, , SD

      d. 20 Sep 1983 Brush, , CO

        (1) **Mark Dee Asper** b. 13 Apr 1943 Mitchell, , SD

        (2) **Jill B. Asper** b. 27 Nov 1950

          d. 3 Jan 1951

     + **Margorie Wight Davis** b. 7 May 1920

      m. 27 Aug 1985

(10) **Russell Eugene Asper** b. 27 Oct 1920 Artesian, , SD

   + **Geraldine Louise Weiss** b. 8 May 1923 Minneapolis, , MN

      m. 8 Dec 1949 Minneapolis, , MN

        (1) **Teresa Louise Asper** b. 29 Apr 1954 Minneapolis, , MN

         + **Joel Peter Anderson** b. 25 Nov 1954 Minneapolis, , MN

           m. 12 Jul 1975 Minneapolis, , MN

             (1) **Norris Fredric Anderson** b. 9 Jul 1982 St. Paul, , MN

             (2) **Liv Augusta Anderson** b. 17 Aug 1987 St. Paul, , MN

(11) **Lorraine Eloyce Asper** b. 20 Oct 1927 Artesian, , SD

   + **Norman Lon Minier** b. 28 Sep 1925

      m. 18 Aug 1949

        (1) **Lon Dow Minier** b. 30 Aug 1950 Sioux Falls, , SD

         + **Gail Ann Riddle** b. 9 Jul 1951 Glendale, , CA

           m. 24 Jun 1972 San Jose, , CA

             (1) **Loran Charisse Minier** b. 28 Nov 1977 San Jose, , CA

              + **Josh Bailey** m. 2 Apr 2000

                 (1) **Andrew Joseph Bailey** b. 31 Mar 2003

             (2) **Clayton Lon Minier** b. 22 Jan 1982 San Jose, , CA

             (3) **Cliff Andrew Minier** b. 27 Apr 1983 San Jose, , CA

        (2) **Tryg Rolfe Minier** b. 14 Jan 1952 Rapid City, , SD

         + **Katherine ElizaBeth Wiley** b. 20 Jan 1957

           m. 17 Aug 1985 Watsonville, , CA

             (1) **Megan Lorraine Minier** b. 14 Apr 1988 Palo Alto, , CA

        (3) **Eric Jon Minier** b. 26 Mar 1957 Loveland, , CO

         + **Kathleen Rose Martian** b. 4 Dec 1961

           m. 27 Dec 1982

             (1) **Brenna Leanne Minier** b. 25 Aug 1990

             (2) **Kayla Michelle Minier** b. 4 Mar 1992

        (4) **Todd Christian Minier** b. 12 Mar 1959 Brownsville, , TX

         + **Dyonnie Kay Stenwall** b. 3 Jul 1961

           m. 20 Sep 1990

             (1) **Larana Lynn Minier** b. 25 Oct 1985

             (2) **Paige Taylor Minier** b. 16 Apr 1995

             (3) **Morgan Nicole Minier** b. 6 Jan 2002

1   2   3   4   5

(---), (---)	3	Cullerton, Robert Demers (Jr.	5
Anderson, ElizaBeth Marie	4	Cullerton, Robert Demers (Sr.	5
Anderson, Guy William	5	Cullerton, Robert John	5
Anderson, Joel Peter	6	Cullerton, Sally Ann	5
Anderson, Kenneth E.	2	Danielle Marie, (---)	5
Anderson, Liv Augusta	6	Davidson, Mary ElizaBeth	5
Anderson, Matthew William	5	Davis, James	5
Anderson, Norris Fredric	6	Davis, Margorie Wight	6
Anderson, Rachelle Louise	5	De Bolt, Glenda Sharon	3
Anderson, Sydney Carole	2	Degalke, Mary Madeline	4
Anderson, William Arthur	4	Dunn, Deborah Lynn	3
Asper, Albert Leo	2	Graysmark, Emma May	4
Asper, Audrey Elaine	2	Graysmark, Robin Edward	4
Asper, Avis Marscella	1	Graysmark, Ryan Spencer	4
Asper, Dale Raymond	5	Gurley, Derinda D.	3
Asper, David Paul	2	Gurley, Russell E.	2
Asper, ElizaBeth Marie	2	Gutowski, June Mary	3
Asper, Ernest Wilbert	5	Hanson, Milda Berthina	1
Asper, Florence Louise	3	Hegstrom, Mary	3
Asper, Hans Theodore	1	Herbert, B. Kaye	2
Asper, Harvey Clayton	1	Holman, Austin	4
Asper, Helen Pauline	5	Holman, Joseph	4
Asper, Janet Lorraine	2	Holman, Lacey	4
Asper, Janice Marie	1	Holman, Mary Clara	4
Asper, Jayne Valere	2	Hoskins, Sarah Jane	3
Asper, Jean Milda	1	Huelsebusch, Keith	2
Asper, Jennifer	3	Huelsebusch, Tara Lynn	2
Asper, Jill B.	6	Huelsebusch, Tyler James	2
Asper, Judy Louise	1	Janzen, Chad	2
Asper, Katherine Betia	2	Karnes, Tracy Lynn	3
Asper, Lennis Larry	5	Krell, Marie	1
Asper, Leo Paul	2	Lane, Breanna Ashley	1
Asper, Lorraine Eloyce	6	Lane, Christopher	1
Asper, Margery Hortense	5	Lane, Melanie Nicole	1
Asper, Mark Dee	6	Leman, Sidney Taylor	3
Asper, Neal Evan	3	Lukehart, Amanda Jane	3
Asper, Paul David	2	Lukehart, Amos Wolfgang	3
Asper, Russell Eugene	6	Lukehart, Blake Allen	4
Asper, Teresa Louise	6	Lukehart, Bocefus Timothy	3
Asper, Vernie Burdette	2	Lukehart, Dainard R.	4
Bailey, Andrew Joseph	6	Lukehart, Daniel D.	4
Bailey, Josh	6	Lukehart, Dillon	4
Brown, Garth	1	Lukehart, Donald Leo	3
Brown, Tess Diane	1	Lukehart, Donald Vernon	3
Burchfield, Patricia June	5	Lukehart, Dustin	4
Byrd, Barbara Jeanette	3	Lukehart, Erik Matts	4
Cook, Lloyd	5	Lukehart, Gerald Dennis	4
Cullerton, Anne Dawson	5	Lukehart, Gloria Adele	4
Cullerton, Clara Anita	5	Lukehart, Gregg Lawrence	3
Cullerton, John Demers	5	Lukehart, Hugh Allen	3
Cullerton, Pamela Marie	5	Lukehart, Jessalee	3

Lukehart, Jody Richard	3	Rae, Roger Merle	1
Lukehart, Moriet Lisa	4	Riddle, Gail Ann	6
Lukehart, Nicholas	4	Rubida, Christine Deanne	1
Lukehart, Paige Jane	3	Rubida, Danielle Alyse	1
Lukehart, Raven Marie	3	Rubida, Darrell Authier	1
Lukehart, Roger Allen	4	Rubida, Denise	1
Lukehart, Rozelind A.	4	Rubida, Dennis Asper	1
Lukehart, Sherie Diane	3	Rubida, George	1
Lukehart, Spencer Otto	3	Rubida, Pamela Avis	1
Lukehart, Taylor	4	Ruml, Helen	1
Lukehart, Timothy Donald	3	Saffery, Darrick Lance	4
Lukehart, Tucker Nicholas	3	Saffery, Diana Jean	4
Lukehart, Vivienne Joy	4	Saffery, John Gates	4
Maack, Roy	5	Sindle, Jimmy	5
Marshall, Darren Lee	3	Sindle, Mitchell William	5
Marshall, Michael Lee	3	Sindle, Nicholas Travis	5
Martian, Kathleen Rose	6	Sjoberg, Eva Anna-Greta	4
Meece, Teri Ann	4	Springer, Cameron	3
Miketa, Edward	4	Springer, Greg	3
Miketa, Lauren Elsie	4	Springer, Trey	3
Miketa, Marley Autumn	4	Stenwall, Dyonnie Kay	6
Minier, Brenna Leanne	6	Stordahl, James R.	1
Minier, Clayton Lon	6	Stordahl, Lesley Jean	2
Minier, Cliff Andrew	6	Stordahl, Lisa Marie	2
Minier, Eric Jon	6	Sweet, Loretta Christine	1
Minier, Kayla Michelle	6	Taylor, Mickey	1
Minier, Larana Lynn	6	Thielson, Cynthia Sue	2
Minier, Lon Dow	6	Thompson, Ruth Elaine	2
Minier, Loran Charisse	6	Threadgold, Adam Lee	2
Minier, Megan Lorraine	6	Threadgold, Carrie Ann	2
Minier, Morgan Nicole	6	Threadgold, Eric Michael	2
Minier, Norman Lon	6	Threadgold, Harlyn Lee	2
Minier, Paige Taylor	6	Threadgold, Harvey	1
Minier, Todd Christian	6	Threadgold, Karli Marie	2
Minier, Tryg Rolfe	6	Threadgold, Laurie Ruth	2
Nuzum, Gary D.	5	Threadgold, Lee Kent	2
Olstad, Diane Marilyn	1	Threadgold, Lou Ann	2
Parker, Chad Jacob	5	Threadgold, Lynn Michele	2
Parker, Kent Edwin	4	Vanderlinden, Linda	4
Parker, Lindsey Renee	5	Voelzke, Vergie	2
Peterson, Bernice	2	Von Raesfeld, Alexandra	1
Peterson, Beverly	5	Von Raesfeld, Courtney Claire	1
Peterson, Mary	5	Von Raesfeld, Jamie	1
Prater, Dennis D.	5	Von Raesfeld, Jason Scott	1
Prater, Derek D.	5	Von Raesfeld, Michelle	1
Prater, Scott B.	5	Von Raesfeld, Myron John	1
Prather, Julia Lynn	5	Von Raesfeld, Zachary John	1
Purdy, Melissa Dawn	3	Wagner, Jayson Tyler	4
Purdy, Tina Marie	3	Wagner, Robert John	4
Rae, Alexis Louise	1	Wagner, Ryan Justin	4
Rae, Nicolas Edward	1	Walters, Sherry Mae Ann	3
Weiss, Geraldine Louise	6	Wiley, Katherine ElizaBeth	6

Hanson-Helmey Geneology

This is the geneology of Milda Bertina Hanson Asper. Her mother was a Helmey and her father a Hanson. They were both born at Grans Prestejeld, Hadeland, Norway. Today it is known solely as Gran, Norway.

Mari Pedersdatter Helmej (Helmey) was born on Jan. 1837. She came to America in 1856 and lived with her brothers in Winona County, Minnesota, until she married Hans Hanson in 1858. She died at home in Hudson on Jan. 12, 1920

Hans Hanson born July 7, 1832. He and Mary moved to Lincoln County South Dakota in 1872 where they homesteaded in Norway Township. He died at Hudson on Feb. 17, 1914.

The following is the line of ancestory of Mari Pedersdatter Helmej:

Peder Iverson Helmeid---born 1738   (a teacher) died---1793
married in 1763 to Anna Christiansdatter---born 1741

Iver Pederson Helmeid---born 1766   (a teacher)

Peder Iverson Helmeid----born 1791
married in 1822 Mari Toresdatter -- born 1803 on Sorum in West Gran

Peder and Mari had five children:
1. Anne Peder's datter--born 1824 on the Helmej Farm married Gulbrand
        Anderson--born 1828
                    Emmigrated to America in1857
    Children: Andrew, Pete, Knut, Martin, Anna and Sara
2. Iver Pedersen Helmej was born 1827 on the Helmej Farm
3. Torer Pedersen Helmej was born 1829 on the Helmej Farm
4. Peder Pedersen Helmej was born 1832 on the Helmej Farm
5. Lars Pedersen Helmej was born 1834 on the Helmej Farm
6. Mari Peder's datter--born 1837 on the Helmej Farm
                Emmigrated to America in 1856 Married Hans Hanson in 1858
        Mari Helmej (Helmey) and Hans Hanson had 8 children:
1. Henry born 1859
2. Peter born 1861
3. Jim born 1862
4. Magnus born 1864
5. Bernie 1865
6. Annie born 1870
7. Nellie born 1875

Hanson-Helmey Geneology

This is the geneology of Milda Bertina Hanson Asper. Her mother was a Helmeyand her father a Hanson. They were both born at Grans Prestejeld, Hadeland. Today it is know solely as Gran Norway.

Peder Iverson Helmeid---born 1738 (a teacher) died---1793
married in 1763 Anna Christiansdatter---born 1741

Iver Pederson Helmeid---born 1766 (a teacher)

Peder Iverson Helmeid----born 1791
married in 1822 Mari Toresdatter -- born 1803 on Sorum in West Gran

Peder amd Mari had five children:
1. **Anne Peder's datter--born 1824 married Gulbrand Anderson--born 1828**
             Emmigrated to America in1857
   Children Andrew, Pete, Knut, Martin, Anna and Sara
2. **Iver Pedersen Helmej was born 1827 on the Helmej Farm**
3. **Torer Pedersen Helmej was born 1829 on the Helmej Farm**
4. **Peder Pedersen Helmej was born 1832 on the Helmej Farm**
5. **Lars Pedersen Helmej was born 1834 on the Helmej Farm**
6. **Mari Peder's datter--born 1837 on the Helmej Farm**
             Emmigrated to America in 1856 Married Hans Hanson in 1858
   Mari Helmej (Helmey) and Hans Hanson had 8 children:
1. **Henry born 1859**
2. **Peter born 1861**
3. **Jim born 1862**
4. **Magnus born 1864**
5. **Bernie 1865**
6. **Annie born 1870**
7. **Nellie born 1875**
8. **Milda Berdette Hanson born Sept 2, 1878 on the Hanson Farm in Lincoln**
      County South Dakota near the town of Hudson She married Hans Theodore
      She married Hans Theodore Asper born July 4, 1877 on Nov. 28, 1902
      Hans and Milda had 11 children:
1. **Avis Marcella Asper born Oct. 29, 1903**   **Lincoln County South Dakota**
2. **Harvey Clayton Asper born April 27, 1905**
3. **Leo Paul Asper born Oct. 22, 1906**
4. **Vernie Burdett Asper born Aug. 10, 1908**
5. **Florence Louise born Sept. 4, 1910**   **Sanborn County, South Dakota on the**
6. **Margery Hortense born July 16, 1912**   **Asper Farm**
7. **Ernest Wilbert Asper born Jan. 28, 1914**
8. **Helen Pauline Asper born Nov. 12, 1915**
9. **Dale Raymond Asper born Oct. 14, 1917**
10. **Russell Eugene Asper born Oct. 27, 1920**
11. **Lorraine Eloyce Asper born Oct. 20, 1927**

Bibliography: Norwegian Writing

NORWEGIAN BOOKS & PLAYS

Author – Sigrid Undset's
Kristin Lavranssdatter:
- I   *The Bridal Wreath*
- II   *The Mistress of Husaby*
- III   *The Cross*

Playwright – Henrik Johan Ibsen
Five Great Plays
- *A Doll's House*
- *Ghosts*
- *The Wild Duck*
- *The Master Builder*
- *Enemy of the People*

AMERICAN books recounting the trials Scandinavians faced while settling the Mid-West

O.E. Rolvaag – *Giants in the Earth* – Epic Classic of Norwegians on the Eastern plains of South Dakota

Wilhelm Moberg – *The Immigrants Series* – Swedish
- I   *The Immigrants*
- II   *Unto a Good Land*
- III   *The Settlers*
- IV   *Last Letter Home*

Later books concerning Scandinavian Settlers:

Garrison Keillor – Humorous description of Minnesota Norwegians
- *Lake Woebegone Days*
- *Leaving Home*

Wallace Stegner – *The Spectator Bird* – Norwegian couple who've been successful in America board a ship to return home to retire.

Herbert Krause – *The Threshers* – Immigrant Farmers in Minnesota

Lauraine Snelling – *Red River of the North* – Norwegian Pioneer Series
- *The Race*
- *A New Day Rising*
- *A Land to Call Home*

World War II
Military Service

WWII
December 7, 1941 – June 6, 1945

Our Three Star Flag

During World War II, the citizens of the United States were filled with patriotism supporting the troops fighting the war both in Europe and on the Pacific fronts. Every family that had sons or daughters in service were so proud of their children they felt they needed some way to outwardly show their support.

A flag was created just for this purpose. It was a rectangle with a wide border in red. The middle was white. On the white, a blue star was affixed for each family member in service. If a service person was killed, it was replaced with a gold star.

The Aspers had a flag in their window with three blue stars! Ernest was in the Navy, Dale was in the Army Air Corps, while Russell was in the Navy Air Corps. Thankfully, all three came home safely, though it took some months for them to once again readjusted to civilian life.

Ernest Wilber Asper

Ernest, The Navy Man

The end of the 30s harbored great speculation that war was imminent so the government reinstated the SSS (Selective Service System) better known as the DRAFT. So, young men across the United States who were 18 years old were required to register for the draft. One could also choose to enlist and by doing so had the choice of which branch of service to serve in. Ernest had a low draft number, but he decided to enlist.

Ernest was the first son to enter service. He was living in Pontiac, Michigan at the time working for General Motors plant on the assembly line. Since he was not married and had no other responsibilities, he enlisted in the Navy. He was sent to Great Lakes Naval Training Center in Chicago for his basic training. Then he was sent to advanced training to become an airplane mechanic.

Chicago—Ernest W. Asper, son of Mr. and Mrs. Hans Asper, Artesian, S. D., was graduated on December 4 from the naval training school for aviation machinist's mate at the Navy Pier here.

Maintaining one of the highest records of his class, the Bluejacket completed a comprehensive 24-week course, which included instruction in assemblying, servicing and repairing airplanes and airplane engines, and the principle and theory of flying.

He has been promoted to the petty officer's rating of aviation machinist's mate, third class. He awaits assignment to the fleet or to a naval shore station.

Bluejackets are selected for the course on basis of their scores on a series of aptitude tests given them while in recruit training.

USS Princeton (CVL-23)

The fourth Princeton was laid down as Tallahassee (CL-61) by the New York Shipbuilding Corp., Camden, N.J., 2 June 1941; reclassified CV-23 on 16 February 1942; renamed Princeton 31 March 1942; launched 18 October 1942, sponsored by Mrs. Harold Dodds, and commissioned at Philadelphia 25 February 1943, Capt. George R. Henderson in command.

Following shakedown in the Caribbean, and reclassification to CVL-23 on 15 July 1943, Princeton, with Air Group 23 embarked, got underway for the Pacific. Arriving at Pearl Harbor 9 August, she sortied with TF 11 on the 25th and headed for Baker Island. There she served as flagship, TG 11.2 and provided air cover during the occupation of the island and the construction of an airfield there, 1-14 September. During that time her planes downed Japanese "Emily" reconnaissance planes and, more important, furnished the fleet with photographs of them.

Completing that mission, Princeton rendezvoused with TF 15, conducted strikes against enemy installations on Makin and Tarawa, then headed back to Pearl Harbor. In mid-October, she sailed for Espiritu Santo where she joined TF 38 on the 20th. With that force, she sent her planes against airfields at Buka and Bonis on Bougainville (1-2 November) to diminish Japanese aerial resistance during the landings a Empress Augusta Bay. On the 5th and 11th her planes raided Rabaul and on the 19th, with TF 50, helped neutralize the airfield at Nauru. Princeton then steamed northeast, covered the garrison groups enroute to Makin and Tarawa and, after exchanging operational aircraft for damaged planes from other carriers, got underway for Pearl Harbor and

Upon graduation from his training school, his first tour duty was on the shakedown cruise on the USS Princeton, a new aircraft carrier. He boarded the ship in New York on July of '43 sailing to the Caribbean then on to Pearl Harbor. An aircraft carrier was an entirely new way to fight a war. One never marched on the ground, or saw the enemy! Instead, planes took off from the flight deck of the carrier then sortied with the enemy in mid-air. When the fighting was done, hopefully with a kill, the pilot would head back to the ship and land on deck. The planes were then put on elevators, lowered to their spaces many stories below the deck. This was where Ernest did his work, to ready or repair the airplanes for their next attack. It was extremely hot and humid in the space where he worked. The Princeton was in the South Pacific crossing back and forth over the equator hence the torrid weather conditions.

This carrier was based where it could encounter heavy action with the Japanese Air Force. Another of the ships assignments was to photograph areas they thought would be the next assault target. The Naval Air Forces goal was to diminish the Japanese air power quickly to end the war. For these efforts the Princeton received nine battle stars.

This ship was the only permanent assignment Ernest ever had. He was at sea for twenty-two months! Finally, he got a leave. He came back to Artesian to see his family, to restore his mind, body and soul after his long sojourn at sea where so many fierce battles had raged.

Only about two weeks after returning home, the news reported that the aircraft carrier, Princeton, had been sunk at sea! What a terrible shock this must have been for Ernest. He knew so many of these men on board so well. He had to be grieving for those unfortunate shipmates and their families.

Ernest started his navy career as a seaman. Shortly before his discharge he was promoted to Chief Petty Officer, the top most rank for enlisted personnel.

He came home to stay for about a year after his discharge. It was a period of adjustment to civilian life and a cleansing of his mind and spirit from his horrendous war experience. Russ also came home so both lived with mom and dad for several months. He said Ernest never discussed any of his wartime experiences with him.

Avis' husband George died in 1950. Ernest moved out to their farm to help Avis. She decided she would take her two boys and move to California leaving the farm in Ernest's care.

This arrangement did not last long as Ernest was not well. He went to the Mayo Clinic at Rochester, Minnesota where the doctors found an inoperable tumor on his aorta.

He waged his own war against this disease for seven years. He died in 1960 at 46 years of age, the first death in our family. He spent those last years caring for his young son, Lennis imbuing him with all the important traits Ernest knew children must learn in their formative years. His wife, June, a nurse, supported their family by working in government hospitals. He died at the Veteran's Hospital in Reno. From there, Ernest took his finally journey home where he was buried in the Mount Pleasant cemetery at Artesian.

Dale Raymond Asper

Dale, Army Air Corps

Dale's situation at the beginning of WWII was quite different from his two brothers'. He was still living in Artesian working as a manager for Quinn's Department Store, a grocery and dry goods emporium. He had married one of his co-workers, Beverly Peterson in July 1940. Since he had these responsibilities, he was reluctant to sign up when the war started. But he also knew he would eventually be drafted. Instead of waiting, he decided to do the choosing.

In 1943, he took a test which placed him in the Army Air Corps Reserve. He was sent to Sioux City, Iowa to take flight training. But this program was aborted; so, he then had the choice of dropping the Reserve and becoming a cadet in the Army Air Corps or joining the regular army. He took the cadet test, passed and was inducted into the Army Air Corps. Basic training started in Miami Beach.

Barracks were in a beach hotel; so life was plush. But this was short-lived. Because Dale did not have at least two years of college, his group was sent to Ames, Iowa for a six-month program, but it lasted only six weeks. They were sent to Santa Ana, California for ground school, next to flight school in Oxnard and Bakersfield and finally to advanced flying in Marfa, Texas. There he graduated and received his wings. He stayed on as an instructor, but that school was soon closed!

Dale transferred to Great Falls, Montana where he ferried planes to Alaska for the Russians, our allies then! He flew to various bases in the U.S. delivering B-17s, the big bombers of World War II. He was next transferred to Reno for training in a C-46, a cargo transport. Then, he went to Nashville for his overseas assignment.

India was the destination, a far cry from the plains of South Dakota. All pilots of C-46s were sent to Karachi, then assigned to Shabu, India near the Himalayas. Their job was to fly supplies over "The Hump" into China to help the Chinese fight the Japanese. The Japanese had been sending fighter planes to intercept the C-46s, but, by the time Dale arrived, they no longer had the air power which meant he could fly his cargo unimpeded. The cargo could be 55-gallon drums of fuel or general supplies for US troops. These American troops were fighting the Japanese all over China in impossibly remote areas.

The C-46s had a three men crew, a pilot, co-pilot and radio operator. The plane held 1300 gallons of fuel, which would get them over the Himalayas and back. Shabu was at an altitude of only 475 feet so that the planes had to ascend quickly. These planes were not pressurized so at 10,000 feet the crew wore oxygen masks. They rarely flew much over 15,000 feet. They used oxygen at night below 10,000 feet to improve their visibility. Since it was

CURTISS C-46F COMMANDO
"CHINA DOLL"

THE C-46 WAS CONCEIVED IN 1936 AND FIRST FLEW ON MARCH 26,1940 AS
A CW-20 PROTOTYPE. INTENDED AS A PASSENGER PLANE, BUT DUE TO ITS
GREAT LOAD CARRYING ABILITY AT HIGH ALTITUDE, IT WAS DRAFTED BY THE
MILITARY AS A HEAVY TRANSPORT. ITS MOST NOTABLE USE WAS HAULING
MEN AND MATERIAL OVER THE "HUMP" FROM INDIA-BURMA TO CHINA
AFTER THE BURMA ROAD WAS CAPTURED BY THE JAPANESE ARMY.
THE USAF AND NAVY (R5C-1) CONTINUED TO USE THE COMMANDO IN KOREA,
AND INTO THE MID 60'S. AIR AMERICA ALSO OPERATED THE
C-46 IN S.E. ASIA DURING THE VIETNAM ERA.
THIS AIRCRAFT Ser#44-78663 WAS BUILT IN JULY 1945 AT BUFFALO N.Y.
AND SAW MILITARY SERVICE UNTIL 1950. AS A CIVILIAN SHE FLEW AS AN
AIRLINER FOR METEOR, RIDDLE, ZANTOP AND ORTNER AIRLINES.
SHE ENDED HER COMMERCIAL CAREER AS AN AGRICULTURAL SPRAYER.
IN 1978 SHE WAS DONATED TO THE CAF BEING ASSIGNED TO THE WEST TEXAS
WING WHO PROMPTLY PAINTED HER IN THE COLORS OF THE CHINA NATIONAL
AVIATION CORPS.CNAC. HER NAME THEN "HUMPTY DUMPTY". IN 1981 SHE
WAS RE-ASSIGNED TO THE SO. CALIF. WING OF THE CAF
WHO, OVER THE PAST SEVERAL YEARS, HAS RE-BUILT AND RESTORED HER
TO MILITARY CONFIGURATION AT A COST OF OVER $150,000.
IN APRIL OF 1985 SHE WAS PAINTED AND RENAMED "CHINA DOLL".
CHINA DOLL IS BASED AT CAMARILLO CALIF. AND TOURS THE
WESTERN STATES TEACHING THE HISTORY OF WWII AIRCRAFT

CURTISS C-46F COMM

ENGINES	PRATT & WHITNEY	R-2800-52	2000 HP ea.
Length	76 ft 4 in	Max speed	253 MPH
Height	21 ft 9 in	Cruise Speed	197 MPH
Wing Span	108 ft	Fuel Cap.	1400 Gals
Empty WT	29,500 lbs	Fuel Usage	175 GPH
Gross WT	48,000 lbs	Range	1700 Mi
Max Ceiling	29,500 ft	Crew	4

THE C-46 WAS THE LARGEST OPERATIONAL TWIN ENGINE AIRCRAFT
IN AMERICAN SERVICE DURING WWII.
THE C-46 MADE HISTORY IN WWII BY FLYING VITAL SUPPLIES OVER
THE HIMALAYAN MOUNTAINS FROM INDIA-BURMA INTO CHINA, THIS
FEAT WAS KNOWN AS "FLYING THE HUMP". OVER 900 AIRCRAFT WERE
LOST IN THE CBI THEATER OF OPERATION.
CHINA DOLL Ser# 44-78633 WAS BUILT IN BUFFALO N.Y. IN JULY OF
1945, AT A COST OF $233,377. OF THE 3181 BUILT, THERE ARE BUT A
FEW FLYING IN THE WORLD TODAY, ESTIMATED TO BE 35.
THANK YOU FOR YOUR SUPPORT AND DONATIONS TO KEEP
CHINA DOLL IN THE AIR.

very cold and the planes' heaters never worked, they wore suits that had electrical wiring that had to be plugged in, just like an electric blanket.

Their flying time was four hours each way. Dale remembers once landing in Kumming (Yunnan). While, their plane was being unloaded, they were driven into town for Chinese food. Dale especially remembers the fresh eggs they were served. If they felt they needed additional fuel, they took on just enough to get them back. It would be a frightening flight knowing you had to get to your home base without running out of fuel. By the time they landed, they had put in a 14-hour day.

These flights were tedious but the pilots were constantly aware of their hazardous courses. They had only basic navigational aids that often didn't work because of the altitude. They flew "dead reckoning" – time-distance-course. They had no protection, no fighter aircraft. They knew they were deemed second-class despite the perilous missions as the war in Europe took precedence over that in Southeast Asia. They had an American flag sewn on their jackets in case they had to crash land. These inexperienced young men dealt with the fear and pressure of their jobs. They lived in a strange country in one of the most isolated parts of the world with a different culture and a language barrier. This must have been overwhelming. Dale flew an incredible 97 missions in those 11 months!

In India, they were housed in large wooden barracks, 50-100 officers to a barracks. Dale didn't like this and made friends with two officers who had a private room. They ate canned foods from the States. For entertainment, they played cards, swam in a pool they had built themselves and danced with the nurses stationed there. On Dale's first R & R, he went sightseeing in the mountains where the natives lived. He went canoeing and remembers thousands of noisy monkeys. On his second R & R, he went up higher in the Himalayas to an English resort. There he golfed and enjoyed the fresh food and luxurious accommodations.

These young men returned to the States in December 1945. Dale was home for Christmas with Bev and Mark and was discharged a month later. He went back to his former job almost immediately and never was interested in flying again!

—As told to Lorraine Asper Minier

Russell Eugene Asper

Russell, Navy Air Corps

WASHINGTON, D.C., December 7, 1941

My roommate, Bob Zieman (a cousin to my brother-in-law George Rubida), and I were reading the Sunday paper and listening to the radio when a special news report announced the Japanese bombing of Pearl Harbor. There were few details as to the damage inflicted, but the news was very shocking to us and we kept buying the EXTRA edition newspapers that were soon on the streets.

It was several days before details were known, as communication was slow in 1941. Even though we knew storm clouds were gathering around the world, and brother Ernest was already serving in the Navy, this surprise attack was totally unexpected. I had a deferment because of working for the FBI, but decided to enlist in the Navy as soon as possible. The sailor who interviewed me saw that I had finished a couple years of college and suggested that I try out for the aviation cadet program. Unlike many young men of the time, I had never really thought about learning to fly, but took his suggestion and was sent to the base at Anacostia, D.C. for a series of mental and physical tests.

Although I was accepted into the program, this was in December and the first class they could get me into was July 2, 1942. I continued working at the FBI and taking classes at George Washington University until it was time to report for duty. I took my primary training at Anacostia, D.C., living and taking ground school classes there and busing about 25 miles into the Maryland countryside for flight training. I managed to pass all the tests in the three months of primary training, flying an N2S, an old bi-wing (double wing) plane.

We moved on to Corpus Christi, Texas, for advanced training. It was a two-day train ride from Washington to Corpus Christi. Most of my classmates were from the East Coast and were in awe of the wide-open spaces of Texas, but being from South Dakota I was used to open space. We progressed through several stages of instruction until we picked a speciality. I choose patrol bombers, so moved back to the main base and flew PBYs, a plane that landed and took off in the water. After passing more tests, I graduated on February 19, 1943.

I was very pleased to have finished in seven and a half months and excited about the future. I was assigned to the Atlantic Fleet for duty, but before reporting, I enjoyed a two-week leave back in South Dakota. While I was gone, the folks had left the farm and moved into Artesian and it was my first visit in their new home. Sisters Margery and Helen came from Butte, Montana, to visit while I was there.

127

After the leave, I reported to Norfolk, Virginia, for assignment. They sent me to the Jacksonville NAS for another three months of training which included PBY5As which had landing gear, enabling the planes to land either in water or on a runway. After completing this phase, several of us returned to Norfolk to wait for assignments. After all this preparation, it seemed like a long wait. We spent many days going to Virginia Beach which was nearby and made a couple of trips to Washington to visit old friends.

Finally, in June, seven of us were assigned to VPB 73 which was located in Port Lyautey, Morocco. This was a patrol bomber squadron whose duty was to protect convoys bringing supplies and personnel from the U.S. There were two veteran pilots from that squadron who were flying two PBY5As back to Port Lyautey, so we seven, along with a Catholic chaplain, rode along. We were routed the northern route, with stops at Goose Bay, Labrador, Greenland, Iceland, Scotland, and southwestern England on our way to Port Lyautey. The trip took nine days. I found Greenland and Iceland very interesting with 24 hours of daylight at that time of the year. It was scary flying up a narrow sea inlet cut into the mountainous coastline of Greenland to find the lonely little airport with a single runway.

Our squadron flew patrols covering convoys coming to the Mediterranean. On July 10, 1943, the Allies invaded Sicily and landed in Italy on September 3. President Roosevelt came through the area for the meeting at Yalta with Stalin and Churchill. Some of us were moved to Agadir, Morocco, where we flew around the Canary Islands checking on the German ships interned there, along with other patrolling duties. One of our planes was hit by gunfire and there were injuries. Spain was a neutral country, but their sympathies seemed to lean toward the Axis.

We got in many hours of flight time, as most flights lasted 10 to 12 hours. There were few navigational aids as we didn't want the enemy to know what we were up to. Coming back after dark, it was no problem finding Africa, but knowing which way to turn was sometimes a problem. One of planes turned

PBY

128

the wrong way one night and by the time the pilots realized their mistake, they barely made it back to the base, running out of fuel on the runway.

In December 1943, our squadron got orders to return to the States, and was assigned to Floyd Bennet Field on Long Island, New York. We departed Port Lyautey on December 26, 1943, this time taking the southern route. We landed on Ascension Island, a volcanic wasteland, on New Year's Eve, where we stayed three days because of an engine problem. I filled in as a fourth at bridge with three army generals who were passing through. On our stop in Liberia, the base was surrounded by a rubber plantation. One of the pilots picked up a spider monkey which was quarantined upon arrival in the States. Many of the planes loaded up on the inexpensive rum available in San Juan, Puerto Rico.

Once on Long Island, we enjoyed spending our days off exploring New York City, but flying out over the ocean was very rough. We had to fly low to see the convoys and it was especially turbulent in the winter. I wasn't too unhappy to get assigned to VPB 63 back in Port Lyautey. There were two crews assigned, and we had to take some special training as our new planes had magnetic airborne detectors (MAD). This gear was supposed to pick up signals from a submarine even below the water's surface. We left the States in June, routed via Newfoundland, through the Azores, to Port Lyautey. We waited several days in Newfoundland until the weather was right. We took off at night and landed on one of the islands of the Azores for refueling.

VPB 63 had only seaplanes, so I had to get used to flying them again. It was a little tricky, as we had to land and take off on a river that wasn't very wide. There was a ship channel so we had to watch out for ships coming and going. Our main mission with the MAD gear was to fly about 50 feet over the water in the Straits of Gibralter to intercept any submarines entering or leaving the Mediterranean. Of course, we could only fly during daylight as it would be too dangerous to fly that low at night.

At the end of December 1944, I was assigned to a detachment going to England as the German UBoats were coming in close to shore and they thought we might be able to help with our MAD gear. On the way up we spent the first night at Marseille, France. The next day was very overcast and we ran into bad weather with icing conditions, and finally dropped down to try to find a place to land. We saw several runways, but they looked too shot up to land on, so we landed on a small lake at Glomel, Brittany. We were warmly greeted by the locals and put up for the night. I decided to stay on the plane, as we were supposed to protect our secret MAD gear. The next morning the rest of the crew came out and the commander said we were taking off even though the weather was still bad. It didn't seem like a very good idea, and it wasn't, as we ran right up the bank, through a hedgerow, and pretty much totaled the plane.

Fortunately, no one was hurt. We then went back into town and were assigned to different homes. Two of us were assigned to the local butter and egg man so we had good food. However, the weather was cold and the only heat the house had, besides the kitchen stove, was a fireplace. We were treated royally every place we went and were invited to dinner at other homes. The family we stayed with had a barrel of hard cider on the back porch which we had with meals. The people suffered shortages of things such as soap and salt, but they were very generous with what they had. We were rescued after about a week – the Navy sent a truck to retrieve the secret gear and I went with the truck to LeHavre where there was a supply depot. From there, I got a ride to Dunkeswell, England, where we were to be stationed. There was about a foot of snow on the ground, and we learned that the storm that had forced us to land in France was one of worst of the century, covering most of Europe. Bandleader Glenn Miller was lost in this storm on a flight from England to France.

I enjoyed my tour of duty in England. Dunkeswell is about 150 miles west of London in Devon County. Shortly before we arrived, Joseph Kennedy, Jr., had taken off from the same field on his ill-fated mission. We had only four planes and I flew with the skipper. He didn't care that much about flying so I was the Patrol Plane Commander most of the time. I enjoyed a five-day pass in London and later another leave in Edinburg, Scotland. We were in England when the war ended.

On the first of June in 1945, about 16 of us took a flight to Paris, coming back the next day. It was a memorable experience, though much too brief. We returned to Africa the very next day and I was assigned one of the old PBY5 seaplanes to fly back to the States. That was a challenge as there was no night landing facilities at Recife, Brazil which meant that you had to make it from Bathhurst, Gambia, to Brazil in about 12 hours. Also, there is always a weather front in the middle of the Atlantic which can be turbulent, making flying difficult. But, obviously, we made it.

With the war winding down, I received a 30-day leave in July and then was assigned to a squadron ferrying planes to the NAS San Diego and to fields in Oklahoma where they were retired from duty. I was discharged just in time to get home for Christmas 1945. Two of my brothers, Dale and Ernest, also served in World War II. I never ran into Dale, but ran into Ernest a couple times in Florida, where he ended up after serving aboard the aircraft carrier Princeton in the Pacific for most of the war.

—By Russell Asper